Power & Towers & Swimming:

The Guide

Also by Jake Shellenberger:

A Tucson Summer

Letters to Chad: Building a Summer League Swim Team

www.jakeshell.com

Power & Towers & Swimming:
The Guide

Jake Shellenberger

Jacob A. Shellenberger

2016

First Printing: 2016

ISBN: 978-0-692-78360-3

Published by: Jacob A. Shellenberger

Cover Design: Jacob A. Shellenberger

Cover Artwork: Meghan Babcock

Interior Design: Victoria Griffin

Editor: Victoria Griffin

www.jakeshell.com

Dedicated to

the many mentors

who have helped me

along the way. Also to

the hardworking, passionate,

and committed student-athletes

I've had the great opportunity

to coach. Your sacrifices

were never taken for

granted, and your

efforts will never

be forgotten.

Fast swimming is most

gratifying when shared.

Contents

Acknowledgements

I would be remiss if I did not take the time to thank the following seven coaches who have guided and mentored me in my young career, coaches from whom I have acquired much knowledge, and for without said mentorship this book would cease to exist. I have learned a tremendous amount about Power Towers and power/sprint training from these seven, and my current beliefs regarding said training is a tree of sorts, with this group as major influences, combined of course with my own theories and thoughts I have spent much time questioning and developing along the way.

First, thank you to Tim Verge, my coach at Shippensburg University. Coach Verge planted a dream in my mind and told me that yes indeed, I could become a sprint coach at the Division I level, and inspired me to work toward said dream despite coming from a humble Division II background and being a poor-to-average swimmer at best. During my first three years at Shippensburg I had no idea that Division I programs had dedicated sprint coaches who worked primarily with a core sprint group, and I was mesmerized by the fact that one could make a teacher's salary while coaching 200-and-under types specifically. When he told me as much I was hooked, and the rest, as they say, was history. Tim, thankfully I turned out to be a better coach than a 200 freestyler!

Many thanks to Frank Busch, Rick DeMont, Greg Rhodenbaugh, Augie Busch, and the University of Arizona, who allowed me to volunteer in Tucson in the summer of 2007 as part of a professional development opportunity in conjunction with Penn State. I was on staff at PSU full-time, while living and coaching in Tucson and learning from some of the best coaches and athletes in the world. It was a dream come true for a young sprint coach when considering the following; the great South African 4x100-Meter Freestyle Relay of 2004-Athens fame was back in the desert training full-time, Arizona was the Mecca of Power Tower training (I nearly passed out when on my first day I counted twenty-four Power Towers on the pool deck), and the collegiate group was elite in their own right (both the men and women would go on to win NCAA Division I team titles the following school year).

Arizona had never won a team title up until that point, and the year after my *Tucson Summer* they won two. Perhaps there was a bit of good swim karma involved in allowing a young sprint coach the amazing opportunity to learn from their elite program. To the young coaches reading this, if you ever get the opportunity to have a similar experience, take it. To the established coaches reading this, if you have the opportunity to give a young coach such a gift, do it. That magical summer in the desert changed my coaching trajectory forever, and I will always be thankful for Frank's kindness and willingness to allow me the opportunity to learn from him and from the Arizona staff.

Fourth, thank you to John Hargis, a former PSU head coach and current University of Pittsburgh head coach, under whom I had the chance to coach in 2008-2009. John is a former Auburn student-athlete, Associate Head Coach, and NCAA champion, having also won gold as a member of the US Men's 4x100 Medley Relay in Atlanta 1996. John swam under the great David Marsh at Auburn, and brought many of the Marsh/Auburn sprint secrets with him to PSU, passing much of his knowledge to me along the way.

And last but certainly not least, a special thank you to Bill Dorenkott, a former head coach at Penn State and current head coach of the Ohio State women's program. Bill hired me away from Division II Millersville University, where I was the head coach, to PSU in the fall of 2006, taking a chance on a young, then-unproven small-time college coach with no Division I experience, and with only a willingness to work extremely hard and the enthusiasm to learn as much as possible to sell to recruits and the Penn State student-athletes at the time. It was Bill who also put in motion the wheels that would land me on the pool deck at Arizona, and it was Bill who played the largest role in my hiring here at Liberty. A great teacher of the sport and a patient, tireless mentor, Bill taught me more about swimming in two years at PSU than I would have learned in a lifetime otherwise. Bill, thank you, you took a chance on me and gave me the one thing that every young coach trying to make it in this sport yearns for, an opportunity. It was this opportunity at Penn State that jumpstarted my coaching career, and for said opportunity I will always be thankful.

To the aforementioned coaches, I owe you many thanks!

Foreword

By Sam VanCura, President, Total Performance, Inc.
Manufacturer of the Power Tower and Power Rack

In the summer of 1998, Jim Steen, the legendary head coach at Kenyon College, visited me in my home. I have been friends with Jim since before the first grade, as we both attended the same grade school and also spent a year together at Kent State University. Jim was an All-American backstroker at KSU under Coach Frank Vichy. Following graduation, Jim went on to coach at Miami University (Ohio) and then on to Kenyon College. Jim has the distinction of holding the most consecutive national team championships in NCAA history in any sport, and also the most national team championships overall, with his Lords and Ladies of Kenyon College winning fifty total NCAA Division III Swimming & Diving team titles.

I took a different path to business, where I became a manufacturer's representative before launching Total Performance, Inc. in 1998. I swam for two years in high school, coached a few summer-league teams, and then followed Jim as the coach of the Mansfield YWCA team in the mid-1970s. Jim and I remain great friends and business partners to this day; we spent eight days hiking in New Zealand last year and are planning another trip for 2016.

Back to that summer day in 1998: Jim, in the middle of a conversation, said, "Sammy, we should start a company and make a Seabreeze machine."

The Seabreeze, as it was known then, was an apparatus that suspended weights from a Tower and connected to the swimmer via a belt and cable. Jim followed up with some literature about the product, which also listed a patent number. I was skeptical about possibly violating a patent and followed up by calling Bob Hopper, whose father invented the Seabreeze for him. Bob was ecstatic that someone had an interest in the product.

Total Performance was launched, and a royalty was paid to Bob until the patent ran out. More than eighty-five improvements have been made to the Power Rack since its inception, and 2014 was the largest sales year for the Power Rack to date. The Power Rack is perhaps the best tool available on the market today for developing sprinting power. The short distance and the fast turnover rate on the Rack trains the ATP-CP energy system to the fullest, and also helps to increase stroking power and easy speed. Rick Sharp, Ph.D., of the Department of Health and Human Performance at Iowa State University, concluded that there was a high correlation between training on the Power Rack and sprinting power in the 100-yard freestyle.

Power Tower

Over the years of selling the Power Rack and our Power Cam underwater mobile video camera, I had become of a friend of Rick DeMont, an assistant, then associate head coach, and now the head coach at the University of Arizona. In the winter of 2004-2005, Rick called me and said that I had to come to Tucson to see a 25-yard Power Rack that he and the Arizona staff had invented. I said that it would have to wait until my high-school team's season was over in February. Rick insisted that I come down so I flew to Tucson one afternoon, took pictures and measurements of the 25-yard Racks the following morning, and flew home that afternoon. Our welder, Tom Tenney, redesigned the machine and we named it the Power Tower. On every Power Tower sold, we pay royalties to Frank Busch, the UA head coach at the time and current National Team Director, to Greg Rhodenbaugh, a UA assistant at the time and now the head coach at Missouri, and to Rick DeMont, making us partners in the venture.

At the suggestion of a friend in the industry we changed the type of pulley, which allowed a price reduction, but turned out to be a disaster, as that specific pulley did not have bearings of any kind, causing incredible friction and a bumpy ride at heavy weights. It was also not a sealed system, allowing for the Tower cords to become tangled if they slipped off the pulley. We think that we have identified all owners of that style and changed out their pulley systems at our cost.

Our earlier models used aircraft cable to connect the swimmer to the buckets. Rob Sleamaker of Vasa Trainer fame introduced us to a marine rope that he uses for the Vasa Ergometer. It is a significantly better product and allowed us to reduce the cost to our customers. I estimate the rope lasts four to five times longer than aircraft cable and significantly reduces the coefficient of friction. We also changed the Power Rack from cable to rope.

The first Power Rack was shipped to Cal Bentz at the University of Nebraska and did not include a shock cord. The stop was so abrupt that we were concerned about back problems. We quickly added a metal spring at the end of the cable. That was short-lived as Chris Hall of NZ Manufacturing suggested that we use surgical tubing instead of the spring. We go through hundreds of shock cords yearly.

We initially had fears that the Power Tower would take sales away from the Power Rack. History has shown that has not been the case. Most coaches realize that the two machines offer different training protocols, and we often get orders for the Racks and Towers from the same program.

We have had some design changes over the years with the Power Tower. The earliest design had the buckets outside the frame in a T design. We changed the framing so that the buckets were suspended inside the frame. The design offered not only better safety, but also allowed the top half to be nested inside the bottom for easier shipping. This reduced the chance for damage during shipping, and as those of you who have ordered a Power Tower know, the nine-foot height of the machine necessitated that it be built in two sections.

The earliest Power Towers paid out 25 yards of cable, and our first order into Canada required a 25-meter model. From that time forward we only built 25-meter Power Towers as more of a one size fits all model, and we have shipped Power Racks and Power Towers to every corner of the globe, from Australia to South Korea and everywhere in between.

Power training for swimming has been a passion for Jim and me for more than twenty years, and we hope you enjoy the Power Tower and Power Rack as much we have enjoyed manufacturing them over the years.

Sam VanCura
December, 2015

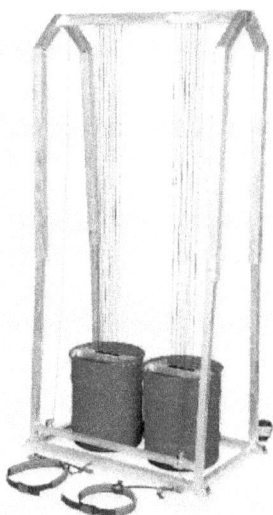 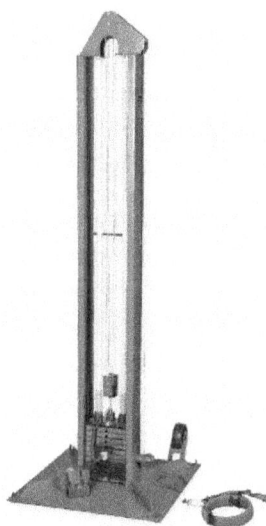

Power Tower   **Power Rack**

Photos courtesy of Total Performance, Inc.

Preface

Lynchburg, Virginia
December, 2015

I have posted many thoughts and pictures on social media over the years, highlighting various Power Tower and sprint-training exploits, both here at Liberty and during my time as the sprint coach at Penn State. It was through these postings and word of mouth that I received quite a few requests via email from coaches throughout the country for Power Tower training advice and general information. After the fifth request and five personalized emails (some totaling more than ten pages in a Word document), I decided to pen this book on power training for swimming and share what I have learned throughout my career, with the hope of inspiring coaches and athletes alike to reach new levels of competitive success and creativity in our sport.

There have been many articles in the swimming world written about sprint training and power training in the general sense, and the two *Sprinting* books by Sam Freas are some of my favorites on the topic. It was Sam's first book, *Sprinting: A Coach's Challenge*, that originally inspired me to become a speed coach, and while it is showing some age, I still have the original copy I bought back in 2002. To my knowledge, however, there are few if any books or articles of any great length or detail devoted entirely to power training specifically; thus, I have set out to write the definitive guide on power training for swimming. While all-encompassing, this book focuses heavily on the Power Tower and its versatility, for it is certainly much more than a toy for pure 50-freestyle and stroke types, as you will see!

In the following pages I will share with you my personal beliefs on the subject and what worked for me at Penn State, where I was the sprint coach from 2006-2009, and what is currently working here at Liberty, where I have been the head coach since starting the program from scratch in 2010. We have had a bit of sprint and overall success here at LU across multiple events in a short amount of time, and we do well taking average swimmers out of high school and training them to be elite level NCAA Division I student-athletes.

I have spent much time contemplating the mysteries of the Power Tower (and resistance training in general) at the Division I level for ten years now, and the following is nearly everything I have learned in those ten years, along with the many unanswered questions I still have for the future of swimming and power training as a whole. I am confident and hopeful that in another ten years my thoughts and beliefs will change and evolve, but for now, the subsequent pages are the sum total of what has worked, and worked well, for me and the programs for which I have had the great opportunity to coach.

Chapter 1: Introduction

"If you want to find out what the capabilities are, you have to use the Towers. You could plan a whole season centered on them."

Rick DeMont
June 5, 2007

SWIMMING COACHES have been using various forms of resistance training for quite some time now, and the evolution of resistance and power training has been steady over the past forty years. While writing this book, I was contacted by Tom Meade, the current master's coach at Binghamton University in New York, who informed me that he had written an article detailing resistance training on an early version of a Power Tower-type device he called the "Swim-on" while working on a Master's Degree in Exercise Physiology at Ithaca College in the 1970s. The article, entitled "A New Approach and Method of Weight Training for Swimmers" was published in *Swimming Technique* magazine in September of 1976. Unfortunately, Tom was unable to secure a patent on the product, and after a few years, the concept evolved into the Seabreeze machine patented by Bob Hopper, referenced by Sam in the opening foreword.

Tom sent me a copy of the article, and it is fascinating to read the concepts and ideas of Power Training from the 1970s. (On a side note, if the reader should be so inclined, the histories of *Swimming World*, *Junior Swimmer*, and *Swimming Technique* magazines are quite intriguing in their own right. Thank you to the legendary Albert Schoenfeld and Peter Daland for their early work in covering our sport, and thank you to Dick Deal for continuing the legacy that is now *Swimming World*.)

In Chapter Five of this book, I will cover drilling on the Power Tower and explore the concept of resistance training improving, rather than degrading technical excellence, but before then I wanted to share with you an excerpt from Tom's article. I am happy to know this concept is nothing new. In the 1976 article, Tom states:

> In analyzing the 'Swim-on' and its programs, it is evident that it builds strength, muscle endurance, and cardiovascular endurance, while increasing flexibility through the intensity, duration and repetitions of the work bouts. The 'Swim-on' program also refined coordination and sensitivity of feel to occur in the swimmer's stroke. This is presently not available in any other program . . . With the added resistance of the weights directly opposing the swimmer's forward motion, errors in technique stand out like a 'sore thumb.' This enhances the coach's ability to pick out and correct errors in technique. The 'Swim-on' allows for automatic correction of errors in stroke mechanics. (Meade 1976, 68)

Imagine a graduate student writing about resistance training improving technique in 1976; to say that Tom was ahead of his time is quite the understatement, indeed. While I will expand a bit on Tom's thoughts in Chapter Five, he got it right forty years ago—resistance training does indeed improve technical excellence under the watchful eye of a competent coach. In writing this book, I found it fascinating to see where we were back then and just how far we've come with regards to power and resistance training in our sport.

As for my own journey into the realm of power training, coming from a humble Division II background, I was limited with regards to resistance training in my swimming career, as we did not use resistance during my time at Shippensburg. My first introduction to using the Power Tower was as the new sprint coach at Penn State, where as mentioned I was hired in the fall of 2006. At that point in my coaching career I had seen Power Towers and Power Racks on various pool decks over the years, though I had never had the opportunity to coach at a program that implemented them in workouts. I was delighted with this training device, and PSU featured four Power Racks, six Power Towers, plenty of weight belts, ankle weights, and even a block in the diving well, and while a small well, was perfect for training sprint types. We later added another six Towers for a total of twelve, and with twelve Towers, four Racks, and the various other resistance devices, PSU had quite the setup for a new sprint coach.

I quickly set out exploring the potential of the Towers and power training in general, both as a coach and personally. Looking back at my own college career and wishing I'd had the opportunity to use resistance, I made up for what lost time I could during my own personal "stay in shape" swim sessions at PSU. I immediately fell in love with resistance training, as I became stronger and simply felt better in the water, and was at once convinced that I would have swam faster at Shippensburg if I'd had the opportunity to use resistance during my collegiate days.

We had great success sprinting at PSU, sending relays to NCAAs and even trained a national champion, and in the 200 backstroke of all events, but as you will see, the Power Towers played a leading role in that achievement, certainly as much if not more so than our success in the 50 and 100 free. I learned much regarding general power and sprint training in my days at Penn State, which included a stop at Arizona as a volunteer assistant in the summer of 2007, and owe much of our current sprint (and overall) success here at Liberty to my Penn State and Arizona experiences.

Ten years later, and now six full years into our program's young history here at LU, I not only still believe in the Power of the Towers, I have grown to love the various benefits of training with resistance even more so than during my days at PSU.

The Power Tower is for everyone, for all distances and all events, not just the 50 and 100 freestyle. As noted, at Penn State we trained a national champion in the 200 backstroke, with Patrick Schirk winning the title in 2008 with a 1:40.22 in Federal Way, WA. He trained on the Towers three times a week, and much to the shock of many in the coaching community (this was well before USRPT became popular), we trained Patrick's 200 back out of our sprint group with a low volume, high intensity approach that featured plenty of resistance, with a mixture of Power Towers, weight belts, ankle weights, cords, Power Racks, and more.

One of my fondest memories of the Power Towers was watching the entire Arizona crew in 2007 work a team power set my first day in Tucson. The Wildcats had a fantastic setup for training power, arguably the best in the country at the time, in my humble opinion, and it is even better now since their recent pool renovation. Imagine a young sprint coach walking onto the deck and seeing twenty lanes, twenty-plus Towers, and the entire team training power, all together, all at once, and all in the same pool. I mentioned to Frank that even the distance swimmers were doing power. He replied, "Yes, Jake, everyone needs power, from the 50 to the 1650."

And I certainly did not doubt him. Here at Liberty our entire team is also on the Towers at least three times a week, from the 50 to 1650, and last year (2015) at our conference meet we had four women place top eight in the 50, three in the 100, three in the 500, and three in the 1650. This year's 2016 CCSA championship featured much of the same, with at least two women top-eight in every freestyle event. While we tend to be more of a low volume, high intensity program, we have range, and our distance crew as stated is still on the Power Towers at least three times a week, all season long, not just a month out from our winter or summer shave and taper championship meet.

Again, resistance and power training is for everyone, and in the following pages, I will give examples of how every distance and every event can benefit from resistance training and specific Power Tower work. While certainly the 50 and the 100 of free and stroke are geared more toward power training from a purely physiological standpoint, I do believe Frank was absolutely correct when he said that everyone needs power, not just 50 and 100 sprinters. Consider Katie Ledecky as one example, with her incredible range from the 100 to the 1500 being a direct result of her tireless work ethic, sure, but also her size, strength, and power. It isn't enough to have endurance—to go 3:56 in the 400 LCM freestyle you need to have raw speed, and Ledecky proved she has the power to hang with the best sprinters in the world with her 52.6 split from Rio. Let me say it once more; power is for everyone, not just the sprint types.

This book is broken down into several chapters, as there is much more to Power Towers than heavy buckets and short blast efforts, and I will outline the chapters on the following pages. Each chapter will have sample workouts and specific sets throughout, some of which are taken from actual workouts during my time at Penn State, Arizona, or Liberty, and I will specify the team, group, and the coach who wrote the set, where applicable.

Some sets are hypotheticals that I created specifically for this book, and having done so I will most likely use them in a future workout. Still other sets are hypotheticals that I may not use, either from a lack of a proper facility or simply not having the courage to do so. I say courage as the upper limits to resistance training in our sport are a great unknown, and it will take a brave coach and a special kind of athlete to fully explore said limits, as you will see.

Throughout, I will also include specific swimming and strength-training literature where applicable to the subject at hand, and I will also infuse a bit of my own personal beliefs. These beliefs may not always align perfectly with the literature, and here we shall see in real time the push/pull that is the art versus science of coaching. There are instances, for example, where the literature says point blank, *this does not work*, but in my ten years I have seen it work time and time again, across three different programs and for a plethora of different student-athletes. One could write a book solely on the art versus science of coaching, across all sports, and while such a work would be a grand and worthwhile project to tackle at some point, for the most part I will keep my thoughts pertinent to the subject at hand for this work.

In Chapter Two, I will outline the benefits and drawbacks to both the Power Tower and the Power Rack, as which piece of equipment to buy is the number one question I have received over the years from coaches looking to get into the power game.

Chapter Three will focus at length on what we refer to here at Liberty as Pure Power, which the reader may find as the traditional power approach of short blast efforts and a high level of resistance.

Chapter Four will focus on what we call Power Endurance, the development of which I believe should be the driving motivation behind the majority of sprint/power training. While yes, even though I am a sprint-minded coach and work directly with our sprint group here at Liberty, I am still of the belief that swimming is an endurance sport (though certainly not in the traditional aerobic sense of the term).

Chapter Five, again, is dedicated to drilling with resistance, and perhaps this chapter above all others will show the versatility of the Tower and its many uses (again the Tower is much more than just heavy buckets).

Chapter Six will focus on the "fifth stroke" and kicking in general, again highlighting the many uses of the Tower and also introducing a training philosophy that while astonishingly simple, has escaped the grasp of an overwhelming majority of coaches for years.

Chapter Seven will touch on the science of power training, and you will enjoy this section if you tend to be more of a technical/science-based coach. I will explore the topics of neural stimulation and Post-Activation Potentiation, and will also explore a bit of the strength training literature, of which there is much to discuss.

Chapter Eight will focus on other forms of resistance, from Drag Sox to weight belts and everything in-between.

Chapter Nine will highlight tips, tricks, secrets, and innovations of resistance training that I believe are specific to our program. This will spill our power secrets so to speak, and while I hesitated to make this a tell-all chapter, I did include nearly everything we may have "invented" here at Liberty.

Chapter Ten was a late addition; I originally planned for ten chapters total, but after writing the book and working through the editing process, I realized that having spoken at length about strength training throughout, I should indeed pen a section specifically on strength training to collect and summarize my thoughts. I come from a strength-training background, and on top of coaching the sprint group at PSU, I also wrote and coached their weight program. This was a unique setup that probably wouldn't be possible in the majority of programs today; I believe we were justified in our reasoning for going this route and the arrangement worked out well for our sprint types.

Finally, in Chapter Eleven, the conclusion, I will address the art versus science of coaching and share my personal thoughts on the matter. I will also dream for a bit and attempt to look as far into the future of our sport as it is possible for me to see. What will the future hold? How will coaches be implementing resistance training, if any, in their programs many years from now? And what of the athletes? Tell me of the first woman to flat start a sub-21-second 50 freestyle, for example. What will her mental and physical characteristics be? What of the first man to flat start 17-anything in the 50 free? Watching Vlad Morozov split 17.86 was a treat, as was Caeleb Dressel's 18.20 flat start 50; these efforts are a glimpse into the future and what kind of athlete, stroke tempo, and stroke length it will take to see a 17-second 50-yard freestyle from a flat start.

In regards to the art versus science of coaching, I do believe there is room in our profession for both science and instinct, if you will, and as with most complexities in life, the sweet spot lies somewhere in the middle, in finding balance and harmony. The aforementioned belief is that of my humble opinion, of course.

I trust you will enjoy reading and referencing this work as much as I enjoyed writing it. This book was an idea whose time had come, as nearly every college program and quite a few high school and club programs train with resistance, whether it be Power Towers, Power Racks, Kevin and Randy Reese's Pinnacle Pulley System, a DIY bucket-device, or some other form not mentioned above.

While there are a few books on sprinting and many that have sections on sprint training, to my knowledge there has not been a work of any great length or detail dedicated specifically to Power Racks, Power Towers, and resistance training in general. I aim to fill that void with this book and to inspire coaches and athletes alike to reach new levels of performance and creativity.

A Disclaimer: There is certainly no one right way to use the Power Towers and resistance training in our sport, and by no means do I claim to have all or even a majority of the answers when it comes to Power Towers, power training, and sprint training in general. I would encourage you to read on with an open mind, taking what you will and what looks interesting and implementing it into your own program, while experimenting to find out what works for you and your athletes and what does not. I am in no way trying to convert coaches to my way of thinking or training; I am simply sharing what I believe and what works for us and our student-athletes here at Liberty. The beauty of our sport is that there is no one right way to train swimmers of all events and distances, and many coaches have found success with vastly different training approaches. For those coaches using a different pulley/resistance system, simply substitute your version for "Tower" anywhere in the book and the method/results remain the same.

Enjoy!

Chapter 2: Power Tower or Power Rack?

"We are thinking about doing even more power this fall."

Rick DeMont
May 30, 2007

As THE most-asked question I have received over the years from coaches just entering the power-training realm, I begin this work with the topic of the Power Rack versus Power Tower. Many of the coaches with whom I have corresponded on this topic were ultimately somewhat disappointed with my response, as I did not explicitly tell them to buy one or the other, no, I simply outlined the many pros and few cons of both and left the choice to them. I did let them know that here at Liberty, we have eight Power Towers and no Power Racks; certainly that fact left them with a good sense of what I thought was best for our program and specific training goals.

I determined early in my coaching career (while on deck at Arizona, specifically) that in my personal opinion, Towers are indeed superior to Racks, and I will share my beliefs as to why in this chapter. My point, however, is not to convince you to choose Towers over Racks, as you may have legitimate reasons for Racks over Towers in specific circumstances; here at Liberty the Towers simply satisfy our training goals and power priorities better than the Racks.

The positives are many, and the downsides are few for both the Tower and the Rack, and coaches will have to weigh the many variables when deciding which piece of equipment to purchase. When determining, here are some questions to ask that will help you in your decision.

What are my power goals? Do I plan on training predominantly Pure Power, Power Endurance, or a mixture of the two?

As we will see in Chapters Three and Four on Pure Power and Power Endurance, respectively, the Power Tower, because of its ability to go as far as 25 meters if one so desires, is the better choice for coaches who want to focus primarily on Power Endurance or a mixture of both Pure Power and Power Endurance. While yes, one could train Power Endurance with repeat 10.5-yard efforts on the Rack, I do believe the 25-yard/meter distance is superior. If, however, you plan on implementing a one-hundred-percent Pure Power-style program, the Rack might be a better option.

What is my budget?

As the Power Tower's overall cost is almost twice that of the Rack, certainly budget concerns will be a thought in the forefront of the minds of many coaches when determining whether to purchase Towers or Racks. While the Tower is technically more expensive, yes, one must remember you are getting two buckets for $2,615 (plus shipping), combined with the ability to have two athletes on the Tower at once. This is not possible with the Racks, as you would need to buy two Racks to do the work of one Tower, negating the cheaper cost of the single $1,695 (plus shipping) Rack.

What facility concerns, if any, do I have?

Oftentimes the facility, or lack thereof, will play a major role in determining whether to buy Towers or Racks. As mentioned, you can train two athletes in one lane on one Tower, whereas with the Racks you are generally limited to one athlete per lane. At Penn State, we did set up two Racks in one lane, but it was crowded, and it lacked the efficiency of the Tower setup.

Here at Liberty we actually use three buckets per lane, with the third Tower splitting the lane line and allowing us to use all eight Racks on one end of our six-lane pool.

Three buckets per lane is possible for short Pure Power-type work, but I would not recommend three per lane for Power Endurance. Two athletes per lane is certainly ideal, and again I'll never forget the first time I walked onto the Arizona pool deck and saw twenty lanes with twenty-plus Towers and the entire program working power at once with two athletes per lane. Beautiful! We just recently announced plans for a new 50-meter facility here at Liberty, with a completion date of July 2017. Once completed, we will increase from eight to twelve Towers and will train primarily in twelve lanes, with twelve Towers, and twenty-four women working the various forms of power together. While not quite the Arizona setup, for a women's-only program, twelve lanes and twelve Towers will serve us quite well.

If facing a similar situation and pressed for lane space, the Towers will offer you the most efficient setup with three buckets per lane, and again, I highly recommend this setup for Pure Power work if lane space is an issue.

How often will I move the Towers or Racks?

Here at Liberty, we currently train in a dedicated REC facility, thus we must store the Towers after every workout. If you have ever had to move multiple Power Racks any significant distance, you will certainly appreciate the ease of moving the Tower in comparison. For us, it is an easy answer, and we have saved quite a bit of time (and frustration) over the years moving Towers in comparison to the significant undertaking that would have been moving Racks. Also, when one again considers the two buckets per Tower and eight Towers total, I cannot imagine having to move the equivalent of sixteen Power Racks each time we wanted to train with resistance (which is often!).

Another benefit to Power Towers in regards to facility issues is that they can be pushed across a tiled pool-deck rather easily in a pinch. While I obviously do not recommend this method as a primary mover, if you're looking for a few inches or even a quick lane change, sliding the Tower across a tiled deck is an option that one would be hard-pressed to mimic with a Rack. An example from a power workout here at LU:

Suppose we are going set featuring station power for our sprint group, three times through, in lanes one through three, with four Towers, and moving the women through the stations as a group instead of "true" stations. That is to say, the entire group would go station one, followed by two, and so on and so forth. In this example, we would not have four different groups with one group at each station.

Stations:

1. 4 X 12.5 Max Blast Kick, odd efforts on the Power Tower (PT) with the bucket filled 1/2 with water, even efforts no PT; all efforts with choice fins

2. 4 X 12.5 or 15 Max Blast Swim, odds going 12.5 on PT with 1/2 bucket, evens going 15 no PT; all efforts with choice of gear.

3. 2 X 25 Cord-Assisted Sprints

4. 1 X 25 Dive max to foot touch, choice flat or relay

We would use lane one for our cord assists, but we would also want one and a half Towers in lane one for the kick and swim efforts. It is quite easy to slide the full Tower in lane one far enough away to safely pull the cord-assist efforts without interference, then slide the Tower back for round two, and so on. Our blocks are on the opposite side of the pool, are obviously immovable, and thus do not let us pull cords from the start end.

This quick moving of the Towers takes mere seconds and is obviously not possible with the Power Rack. As an added benefit, the student-athletes can also safely slide them; this is useful if a coach is not in the immediate vicinity and a Tower must be moved.

To further help with the comparison, I have compiled a quick pro/con list for both the Tower and the Rack. There are arguably many more pro/cons I have not listed; the following are the specifics that apply to our program and help to outline just a few of the reasons we have chosen Towers over Racks:

Power Rack Pros

1. Can accurately measure power output with a stopwatch and the dedicated weight system
2. Feature much more efficient and stronger pulleys than the Tower (more on pulleys to come)
3. Lower total cost

Power Rack Cons

1. Much heavier than the Towers
2. Harder to move than the Towers
3. Smaller maximum resistance load possible
4. Shorter maximum distance (10.5 yards vs. 25 meters)
5. Can only train one athlete per lane
6. Higher cost, per capita

Power Tower Pros

1. Can train up to 25 meters
2. Much lighter than the Rack
3. Easier to move than the Rack

4. More efficient than the Rack if lane space is an issue—can safely go three buckets per lane if one so desires

5. Can go heavier than the Rack, then add weight to the bucket if you want to go heavier still

6. Per capita, is cheaper than the Power Rack

Power Tower Cons

1. The Harken pulleys for the Power Tower are unsealed plastic pulleys that wear out quickly.

2. The pulleys must be replaced often to ensure smooth and efficient resistance.

3. Harken will not make a better pulley of this exact size.

With regards to the pulley situation, it is my humble opinion that the only downside to the Power Tower is the Harken pulleys. Here lies an incredible business opportunity for the mechanically inclined: develop a sealed, steel-ball-bearing pulley of the same size as the current Harken Power Tower pulleys, then sell direct to Sam as the official supplier of pulleys for Total Performance, Inc. There are thousands of inferior pulleys on hundreds of Towers in the swimming world that should be replaced, and I dream of the day when I can replace every pulley on our eight Towers with a stronger, more efficient version.

In closing, when looking at the pro/con list and considering our facility, the Towers are by far the better option for our program. We can train sixteen women on eight Towers on one side of our six-lane pool, and we can train our entire team of twenty-four if a few of the women switch off the Tower quickly once they have completed their efforts and let other athletes have at it. With the Towers, we can train a good mixture of Pure Power and Power Endurance, and the versatility of the Towers over the Racks is reason enough to favor them, in my humble opinion. Not only can one train Power Endurance with 25-yard or meter efforts, the Towers also allow a heavier 12.5-yard effort than the Racks, which is great for Pure Power, as we will see in the next chapter.

The Towers are much easier to move, and I believe they are safer overall than the Racks. When looking at the total number of athletes able to use them at once, they are less expensive than the Racks, and athletic directors will love to see the efficiency when making such a large purchase.

While yes, it is quite the undertaking to fill and refill sixteen buckets with water three to four times a week, I enjoy this part of the job at the sub-conscious, cellular level. I grew up on a ten-generation family farm in Lancaster County, PA, and manual labor was so interwoven into farm life over the past two hundred seventy years of our family's history that it is perhaps engrained into my genome. As I am now off the farm and into higher education, I do enjoy getting back to my roots and filling up several twenty-gallon drums a few times a week; it is great exercise and reminds me of the values and work ethic whence I came.

Having said as much, while we prefer the Towers, there are certainly specific circumstances in which a Rack might be favorable to a Tower, and one such example was my own collegiate experience at Shippensburg. We did not have the equipment budget for Racks or Towers, and any fund-raising went to bolstering our athletic aid, as we were not funded well from a scholarship standpoint. If, by chance, we had gained an extra $1,600 in equipment money or could have fundraised for said amount, it would have been nice to have one Power Rack at the minimum, and I believe it would have helped our program immensely.

If you happen to have an extra $1,600 in your equipment budget and are facing a use-it-or-lose-it situation, by all means, coach, go with a Rack and start with one; you will not regret it, and one Power Rack is certainly better than none at all. As I come from a humble Division II background, I can relate, and your athletes will appreciate (or should appreciate) the opportunity to train on such a fine piece of equipment.

Chapter 3: Pure Power

"Everyone needs power, from the 50 to the 1650."

Frank Busch

OUR SECOND topic will focus on what I refer to as Pure Power, and as the name implies, this is the traditional power training that comes to mind when one considers the Power Rack and Power Tower for a power-focused practice. I begin the training section of this work with Pure Power, as it is the most requested of the various power training topics in the emails I receive, and it is certainly the most fun (and in some cases the most challenging) type of power training for both athletes and coaches alike, and especially for sprint types.

Our entire team here at Liberty works Pure Power at least once a week, and while yes, Pure Power is more geared toward sprint types, it is my belief that athletes of all events and distances can improve raw speed with heavy buckets and Pure Power training. Everyone needs and can benefit from more speed and power, and even the most diehard of distance coaches and those who love the high-volume approach must concede that yes, in order to keep getting faster, one must at some point have a higher top-end speed from which to train their endurance and back-end speed.

Once we transition into a normal training week here at Liberty in early October, we have our entire team on the Towers in some way, shape, or form at least three times a week, and yes, our 500 and 1650 types are going a few Pure Power efforts as part of their protocol at least once a week, as previously stated. While the distance group's focus is primarily on Power Endurance training when it comes to Towers, they can and do go quite heavy on Pure Power efforts, and they love to mix it up against the backdrop of their distance workouts (and to compete against the sprint types for heavy-bucket supremacy in the process!).

The only special consideration I should mention when examining Pure Power for different events and distances is that of breaststrokers, as the breaststroke kick is already quite unnatural for the knees and can be hazardous against heavy resistance. Not only do our breaststrokers swim with a lighter bucket, we make sure they are loose and ready to go before kicking breaststroke with heavier loads. I should note that often it is not that our breast types couldn't go heavier, more so that they shouldn't. We have had some breaststrokers go extremely heavy buckets over the years, and while there are some who can handle the force exerted on the knees and groin muscles, this certainly is not the case for all.

Characteristics of Pure Power

I define Pure Power by the subsequent criteria, although I would not consider these rules to be set in stone and will point out to the reader various cases in which we may maneuver around the guidelines. I imagine every coach using Towers or Racks prescribes some form of Pure Power, and while the specific principles may differ slightly from program to program, I am confident that the reader will recognize Pure Power as I describe our version below.

First, @LUSwimDive, our Pure Power workouts consist of 12.5-yard or 15-meter efforts. On rare occasions, we may go 10 yards, or rarer still stretch the range to 25 yards; however, the overwhelming majority of our Pure Power efforts are centered on the 12.5-yard and 15-meter distances. I prefer 12.5 yards and 15 meters for a myriad of reasons, chief among them:

1. We have a black line across the bottom of our pool here at Liberty at exactly the 12.5-yard mark, and it is astonishing at times how just a simple black finish line can elicit greater efforts during workouts. Never mind the desire to score more points at the conference meet, go a best time, or earn more scholarship money. In some cases, the black line trumps all as a powerful motivator. I am sure the psychology textbooks could pinpoint exactly why a finish line works so well, and I have no doubt there is sound science behind this phenomenon. While I will not get into the science here, a finish line works. This much I know.

2. I believe 15 meters is ideal for butterfly and backstroke types as they can work their underwaters off the wall and still have plenty of water left to take meaningful strokes that will produce the desired physiological changes in the body.

3. I have found that 12.5 yards for freestyle and breaststroke types is the perfect distance to load the Towers with heavy buckets, yet still allow the athletes to maintain some form of adequate, but perhaps not ideal, technique. There is a fine line with technique and Tower work, and while my beliefs regarding such matters are controversial, I do believe I defend said beliefs with sound logic and reason. In short, we do allow for technique to deteriorate in order to complete the 12.5 or 15, within reason, and I will explain why in-depth in the following pages.

Secondly, our Pure Power work is always written by our coaching staff as requiring 100% maximum, all-out effort from our women, and if we ever deviate from 100% max it because we happened to have an off effort; it was certainly not something that was suggested by the coaching staff! If the efforts are not written as all-out 100% maximum, we do not consider it Pure Power work and would most likely categorize the efforts under drilling/technique work or Power Endurance.

Third, Pure Power work here at Liberty features a high load and a high rest-to-work ratio—a high load relative of course to the distance prescribed, the gear used, the stroke chosen, the ability and talent level of the athlete, and the time of year we are prescribing the set. Heavy buckets are, for lack of a better term, quite subjective, and what is heavy for an elite senior sprint freestyler with four years of weight-room and Power Tower experience in our program is certainly going to be different than what is heavy for a freshman who has never trained with resistance in her career.

In short, Pure Power is heavy and would be applicable to maximum-strength work in the weight room, featuring low reps, high weight, and a focus on eliciting specific training adaptations in the neuromuscular system. These adaptations include, but are not limited to, an increased rate-of-force production, an increase in motor-unit and muscle-fiber recruitment, and a decrease in the inhibitory effects of the Golgi tendon system. The overarching goals of Pure Power work are to recruit as many fast-twitch muscle fibers as possible, to train them to produce as much force as is humanly possible, and to do so as quickly as possible. I will address these goals in more detail in Chapter Seven on the neuromuscular system and Post-Activation Potentiation.

Jake Shellenberger

Regarding the weight room and the similarities with Pure Power work, without getting too deep into the strength-training literature, we know much about the basic strength-training adaptations regarding motor-unit and muscle-fiber recruitment, and I do believe the same types of adaptations take place in the pool using Pure Power training techniques. One major benefit to in-water resistance work is that it largely adheres to the principle of specificity, in that we are training movement and recruitment patterns that closely mimic those used in an actual swimming race. There are some who disagree, stating that movement and recruitment patterns are changed slightly when using resistance, and I will address those concerns in the following pages.

One could say then that Pure Power is a way to train "new speed" into the body. Speed is largely a neuromuscular phenomenon, and Pure Power is specifically aimed at training the neuromuscular system. Again, I see Pure Power and training with heavy loads in the pool as having a direct relationship to the weight room, and I do believe the basic components of speed can be trained, and trained well, with the use of heavy resistance in the pool.

Pure Power Season Planning Considerations

Short Course (September - March)

We will transition into a normal, "regular," training week here at Liberty by mid-fall, and we start our Pure Power work in early October each year. This is always a joyous time for our women, as Power Towers are new for the majority of the freshmen, and for the returners it will have been since late July when they last tasted the heavy buckets. I should note that early October is not a hard date, as in some years we have started Pure Power as early as late September. I believe this is largely athlete-dependent, as in most cases juniors and seniors can pick up Power Towers in September where they left off in their July taper without issue. Freshmen in most cases require a longer adaptation phase before they start Tower work, and especially so if they have never trained with in-water resistance in their club or high-school programs.

After starting our Tower work, we will use the first one to two weeks of two to three Tower sessions per week (again athlete-dependent) for general adaptation, before progressing into a classic Tudor Bompa schedule of periodization for the remainder of the season. The major difference here is that we will not test for a one-repetition maximum Tower effort to determine the athlete's max bucket load in order to work off percentages, as many in the strength-and-conditioning world would advise.

I have generally disagreed with the strength-training philosophy on this topic and would rather not see freshmen with little-to-no weight-room experience going for true 1RM lifts in the first two months of matriculation, even after a classic, general physical-preparation stage. The same holds true for early-season Power Towers, and while a freshman could load up the bucket for a 1RM max attempt in early October, I do not believe it means that she should.

A note regarding the load measurements for the buckets of the three programs where I used Towers, Liberty, Penn State, and Arizona: we use (d) water in the Power Tower buckets instead of weights. This is certainly a matter of personal preference on the part of the coaching staff, and we use water here at Liberty for the following reasons.

1. Water is inexpensive. With eight Towers and on our way to twelve, it would be quite expensive, indeed, to outfit all sixteen and then, one day, twenty-four buckets with enough weight plates to elicit the aforementioned neuromuscular stimulation we desire.

2. Ease of movement. Again, we are guests in a rec facility here at LU, and we must move the Towers to and from storage before and after each practice. This is a much more fluid process with water (ha!) as it can be dumped back into the pool prior to storage. I would not want to move the Towers with weight in them as it would wear out the pulleys faster, and we would have nowhere to store the weight plates on deck even if we so desired.

3. We do not measure power output on the Towers and thus do not have a need for exact loads. We simply use 1/3, 1/2, 3/4, full, and full++ buckets to communicate the load for the women so that they know what to expect for a certain set.

The starting bucket load, then, for early season Pure Power is again dependent on the ability and experience of the athlete, as our stronger, more experienced women can start their Pure Power work with the bucket filled 1/2 quite easily, for example, as this load might only be 30-50% of a 1RM effort if they "max out" at a full bucket or more. Consider a weight room comparison: even after a four-week summer break, a strong, experienced athlete could come back in September and start strength training at 50% of a 1RM or more without much trouble (and probably higher).

Our load progression is, of course, also heavily dependent on the ability of the athlete. Some can progress to heavier buckets with ease in a short amount of time, while others take longer for increased load adaptation. Sleep, diet, stress factors, and other lifestyle behaviors and influences will play a major role in this progression, as will our current weight-room training cycle and level of neuromuscular fatigue.

We take into consideration all of these factors and more when deciding how quickly to progress our women to heavier buckets, and two weeks at a given water level is normally enough to produce the desired strength gains and adaptations for those starting out with lighter loads.

Our basic philosophy, then, is to follow a plan similar to what one might find in the weight room with regards to sets, reps, load, etc. For a junior who is advanced on the Tower, with a 1RM of a full bucket or more, and who is also advanced in the weight room, we might go the following bucket load, by week:

October - 50% / 50% / 75% / 75%

November - 75% / 75% / Full / Thanksgiving

December - 50% / 75% / Full / Full

January - 75% / Full+ / 80% / Full++

February - 50% / 33% / Conference / 75%

March - 50% / 33% / NCAA

The number of sets and repetitions prescribed per week will vary depending on the load and the goal of the workout, and I will give examples at the end of the chapter in the Pure Power sample sets. As for the periodization for sets and reps over the course of the season, while we do keep track of total Pure Power volume, the primary measurement is that of the load, as our volume stays relatively flat throughout the year. I realize this is at odds with the classic Bompa theory, but with the high rest intervals required and a two-hour practice time, there is only so much volume we can achieve. As such, we have found that varying the load throughout the year is much more advantageous and efficient than varying the overall volume.

I hesitate to extrapolate the aforementioned season-planning example to cover our entire team, as this specific routine might be the prescription for just one individual athlete. As we know, our sport varies significantly from one person to the next, and we tweak the above baseline depending on a whole host of different physiological factors, many of which I identified previously. As for the championship season, later in this chapter I will discuss my thoughts on tapering the Power Tower work for both the SCY and LCM season, as I believe the end of the year and getting it right warrants a section of its own.

Long Course (April - July/August)

The Pure Power LCM season planning mirrors that of the SCY season, albeit shorter overall, with a shorter adaptation period to start the year. We take a two-week break here at LU after NCAAs, and two weeks allows us, for the most part, to get right back to training in April with a bit higher volume and intensity than we would in early September for the short-course season. In turn, we start our Pure Power work earlier, and the same LCM season for the above NCAA Qualifier might look similar to the following loads, focusing at the end of the summer on US Nationals in August:

April - 50% / 50% / 75% / Full

May - 75% / 75% / Full / Full+

June - 75%/ Full+ / Full++ / 75%

July - Full / 75% / 50% / 33%

August - Nationals / Off / Off / Off

September - Off / Off / Off / Off

While Power Endurance is a bigger focus for us in the LCM season, as you can see, we still challenge our women with high-epercentage loads for Pure Power in the summer. Without the added stress of classes (many take summer classes, but certainly not fifteen to eighteen credits) and with our ability to train LCM outdoors (we currently rent an outdoor 50-meter pool in the summer here in Lynchburg), the summer is perhaps the best time for us to seriously push the limits of the Towers, as, from a purely physiological standpoint (stress, sleep, sun, diet, etc.), we are at our best.

Recovery Considerations

Pure Power is extremely taxing on the neuromuscular system, and a coaching staff must seriously consider recovery when planning and implementing Pure Power work with heavy loads into their training program. First and foremost, let me again quote Rick DeMont from my days at Arizona: "You have two variables . . . volume and intensity. You can have one or the other, but you can't have both . . . if you want both, welcome to sled dogs."

"Sled dogs" was a term that Rick used often to describe a swimmer who had a lot of endurance but not a lot of speed. As coaches, we are well aware of what happens when we ask too much of our athletes from both a volume and intensity standpoint, and in all but perhaps the most elite levels of our sport, a coach will have to choose on which side to err. Here at Liberty we are definitely more of a low-volume, high-intensity program (certainly with our sprint types), and we believe in a lower-volume and higher-intensity approach for our distance women as well.

As a reference point, it is rare that our distance group will top 70k in any given week during the year, and our sprint group has topped 55k in just two years of the six complete seasons of our program's young history. Both of these max-volume weeks were during Florida Christmas training and included LCM workouts in the mix.

What we lack in volume we certainly make up for with intensity, and we ask our women to go max, all-out efforts quite often, with three to four Power Tower sessions per normal training week, with at least two being heavy buckets with a specific Pure Power and/or Post-Activation Potentiation focus. Again, this style of training is taxing on the neuromuscular system, and it is often a challenge for our women to get up and swim fast in-season. The neuromuscular fatigue is magnified by the addition of three weight sessions and two dryland sessions per week, with the two dryland sessions for our sprint types featuring an in/out-of-water power circuit with heavy medicine balls and explosive resistance work. If The University of Florida has the model volume program, I would have to guess that we are at or near the top end in intensity.

The results, however, and the supercompensation effect from the neuromuscular system during taper are well worth the in-season fatigue, in my humble opinion. Our focus is our conference championship meet, and this approach has served us well over the past six seasons. Consider, for example, our best in-season 200 free relay times compared to our conference championship times over the last six years to give you an idea of just how taxing this type of work can be. I should note that we do not suit up at our mid-season invite meet, but the drops are impressive, nonetheless:

2011 - 1:39.92 - 1:34.64 (first year in program history)

2012 - 1:35.92 - 1:31.36

2013 - 1:35.37 - 1:30.01

2014 - 1:34.97 - 1:30.94

2015 - 1:34.94 - 1:30.29

2016 - 1:34.66 - 1:31.08

Our 200 Medley Relay has followed a similar pattern of drops, and again these large time drops highlight the incredible fatigue that Pure Power work can elicit in-season and the need to focus on recovery wherever and whenever possible. Proper sleep, diet, and stress management must be systematically addressed, and educating the student-athletes on the proper protocols of the above three should be an emphasis of any program that chooses to implement Pure Power and heavy Tower loads.

2011 - 1:52.66 - 1:46.56

2012 - 1:46.82 - 1:43.75

2013 - 1:43.68 - 1:39.90

2014 - 1:42.90 - 1:37.80

2015 - 1:44.50 - 1:39.73

2016 - 1:44.42 - 1:39.37

The point, again, is that Pure Power is taxing on the neuromuscular system, and if you implement Pure Power fully into your program with heavy buckets you may not see a lot of "pop" in the stroke or top end speed until you rest the system fully.

In-season, our sprint group follows the training plan outlined below, and recovery, again, is crucial; we do want to swim as fast as possible in dual meets while still focusing on the conference meet. This is a challenging balancing act for every coach, as we must weigh the desire to swim fast in-season with the desire to swim fast at conference and NCAAs. While, yes, I do believe it is possible to do both and to do both well, if and when we err here at Liberty we choose to err on the side of swimming fast at our conference meet, thus it is not uncommon to see us going full buckets or more the week of, and possibly the day of, a dual meet. The three rows—a.m., p.m., and directly following a p.m. workout:

M.	T.	W.	Th.	F.	S.
Aerobic /Kick	Off	Power	Off	Power	Lift/Dive Quality
Power	Race Pace	Dive Quality	Recovery	Race Pace	
Dryland	Lift	Dryland	Lift	Off	

The Wednesday-morning power session is normally a recovery/drill session, and I will outline our Power Tower drilling in detail in Chapter Five. Thursday is an in-water, full-recovery session, and many days our Thursday weight-room workouts also fall more on the recovery side, featuring heavy doses of soft-tissue work and few movements if any above the 80% load. Tuesday and Friday p.m. workouts feature traditional race-pace training or Dr. Brent Rushall's famous Ultra Short Race-Pace Training, while Wednesday and Saturday quality sets feature pure lactate-tolerance work in the form of traditional stand-up dive work or broken efforts from the blocks.

In short, if implementing Pure Power into your training program, recovery must be a focus, and not in speech only. For example, we are not afraid to spend the entire workout on Thursday at a heart rate below 120, with no "hard" strokes and certainly nothing fast. We also talk at length about recovery out of the water, and this is perhaps the great "X-factor" in program design and how much fatigue the neuromuscular system can handle. If your athletes are not taking care of their bodies outside of the pool and classroom and doing everything in their power to recover, there is only so much Pure Power work they will be able to handle.

Proper sleep, diet, and stress management are key, and all three should be addressed at every program, of course, but especially if a high-intensity approach is taken in the water and in the weight room. If there are any lifestyle choices that will sabotage recovery of the neuromuscular system and, in turn your quest for a high-intensity, Pure Power approach to training, lack of sleep and excess alcohol consumption are at or near the top of the list. Consider the hormonal effects alone—both lack of sleep and the consumption of alcohol lowers testosterone and HGH production, and I cannot think of a worse prescription for success when attempting to go heavy buckets at least two times a week for eight months out of the year, especially for women, who need all the testosterone and HGH they can legally summon.

We are fortunate, here at Liberty, to have a campus culture and lifestyle that is conducive to aiding in the recovery of neuromuscular fatigue, perhaps more so than any other university in the country. Consider the following: our students are required to live on campus for their first two years of school, and for those living on campus we have a 12:00 a.m. curfew. There are no "lights out" rules, but students do have to be in the dorms by midnight. Alcohol is heavily discouraged here, with severe penalties for those caught drinking underage, and alcohol consumption is also highly discouraged even if the students are twenty-one or above and living off-campus.

As such, by and large, our women are not out late and are not drinking heavily during their time here at Liberty, and I am thankful since this allows us to fully test the limits of this Pure Power training style. I do not believe we could train the way we do if excessive alcohol consumption were part of the equation, and I would certainly alter the training signifi-cantly if I were at a different university, where I knew the student-athletes were consuming alcohol regularly and, at times, to excess.

Recovery is a must, and I believe we, as coaches, should do what we can to curb the binge-drinking culture found at nearly every university in the country. If we are serious about fully exploring the limits of human po-tential, it is imperative that we do so. Yes, we have proven we can swim fast in spite of the lifestyle choices our student-athletes make. I dream of how fast we could have been if, as a whole, we had slept a bit more and had drunk a bit less. When you hear Matt Grevers, Nathan Adrian, Natalie Coughlin, and other professionals talking about recovery and the intense focus on taking care of their bodies now that they are professionals . . . imagine if that attitude were also a part of the training regimen of current college athletes.

Consider Michael Phelps and his year-long commitment to stay dry until after Rio, then watch the interviews in which he talks about how good he feels now that he is not drinking. Would Phelps have won the 100 fly at Olympic Trials in 2016 if he had not been dry for several months prior? Perhaps, but hearing him talk about how races hurt much more at thirty-one than they did at twenty-three and how every detail of recovery needs to be perfect leads me to believe that no, he would not have won that 100 fly without his newfound commitment to recovery. As for college athletes as a whole . . . a coach can dream!

Taper Considerations

We subscribe to the classic three-week taper philosophy here at Liberty, and we have found this to be the near-perfect amount of rest, while al-lowing us to finish races from the 50 to the 1650. Taper, as we know, is highly individualized, and I will speak in general terms regarding Pure Power taper considerations as on the whole; it is much more personalized than regular-season training.

As mentioned previously in the season-planning section, we max out the heavy bucket efforts the last week of January and then rest for three weeks leading into our conference championship meet. As our conference meet is always held the third weekend of February, we consider the week of the meet our third week of taper. The final week in January is the last time we will let the majority of the women go for max load bucket attempts, with the Full++ bucket weight referring to a full bucket plus additional weight, be it five-pound ankle weights, a ten-pound weight belt, or more. Our Power Tower record for a Pure Power max effort is held by 2015 graduate Meghan Babcock, who went a 15-meter effort with a full bucket and forty pounds of additional ankle weights and weight belts and did so on a Tower with worn-out pulleys that was certainly less than optimal from a drag coefficient standpoint. As it were, Meghan is also a highly accomplished artist and painted the picture of the Power Tower, oil on canvas, that graces the cover of this book. For those of you who know Rick DeMont . . . he certainly would be proud!

Assuming our example in the aforementioned season plan is a stronger athlete who could max at a full bucket or more, the first week in February we would drop to a half bucket, with a farther drop to a third in the second week. It is highly impressive, for lack of a better term, to see the speed and power in the efforts when a bit of rest is introduced, and the athletes drop to the half and then to the third bucket. Our 12.5-yard and 15-meter efforts with a half bucket look as though a regular one third bucket effort during the year, and in the second week of rest the one-third-bucket efforts look more similar to free swimming with no resistance than an effort against resistance. If the Power Tower cord were invisible to the eye one would not even think the athletes were attached to resistance, they are moving so fast!

If our example was a freshman who maxed out during the year at 75%, we would drop to 40% or so for the first week and below 33% for the second week of taper. We tend to follow the model of dropping to half of her max for the first week and then half of that for second, and again we have found this formula to elicit fantastic drops during the third week at the meet. The neuromuscular system is fully recovered by this time, and one can see as much from the relay drops referenced in the previous section. While I cannot prove the following, I believe fully that the neuromuscular fatigue generated by this training style is more taxing on the body than a high-volume approach, and, as such, also elicits a greater supercompensation effect and, in turn, greater time drops when fully rested.

If any athletes desire resisted efforts during the third week of the taper, it would be at 25% or less; this load is not heavy enough to elicit any of the aforementioned goals of Pure Power training responses from the neuromuscular system, and for most this is simply a mental hack, as they feel better staying on resistance a bit longer.

I should note, again, that the Pure Power taper is highly individualized, and we have had athletes over the years who wanted to go heavier buckets longer into their rest. While we certainly would not prescribe heavy loads a week out from our conference meet, if an athlete truly believes it will help them, it is hard to argue against such a belief. Perception as we know is reality to the college athlete, and whatever keeps them stress-free and smiling during taper is the right taper prescription, within reason of course.

At this point we could diverge into a number of topics concerning muscular strength, muscular power, stroke tempo, stroke length, rate-of-force development, technique, and other components of speed that are directly affected by heavy loads on the Power Tower. Without getting too deep into the science of heavy Tower work I will address some general thoughts and beliefs that I have developed over the years.

Pure Power General Thoughts

Getting back to Pure Power and in-water strength work, I do believe that resistance work in the pool increases muscular strength and power, and does so in specific recruitment and movement patterns that mimic those used in free (untethered) swimming. With an increase in strength, we also see an increase in muscular endurance and the capacity for said endurance, and I will address this further in the next chapter on Power Endurance. As a quick example, refer to the classic 225-bench-press, maximum-reps test performed at the NFL Combine. Instinctively, we know that a football player with a 500-pound one-repetition-maximum bench press will be able to press 225 for more repetitions than a player with a 250-pound one repetition maximum. I do believe the same principle applies to swimming, and the stronger athlete will have a larger "base" of strength to apply specifically to Power Endurance.

I do not believe that Pure Power work must always be performed at race-specific tempo when developing maximum strength is the goal. Consider, again, the weight-room comparison, in which the heavier the load, the slower the athlete will move the bar, across all lifts and all movement patterns. There is a wide body of research in the strength-training world regarding this topic, and one belief is that the intent to move is as just as important as how fast the bar is actually moving, specifically when maximum strength is the goal.

For example, it is a physical impossibility for an athlete to move a 90% load as fast as he or she would move a 60% load, but we know that to recruit as many motor units and muscle fibers as is possible to recruit, and to fully train the neuromuscular system, we must stress the body with loads at the 90% range and above. Again, my intent is not to get too deep into the strength-training literature, but having mentioned maximum-effort lifts in the weight room, I would encourage those wanting to learn more to research Alexander Prilepin and his contributions to the Russian strength-training programs of the 1970s, and then move on to how Louie Simmons has incorporated and improved upon the Prilepin method at Westside Barbell using his maximal-effort method.

In order to build absolute maximum strength, the strength-training literature is adamant that one must lift near-maximal loads at 90% or above, and this will obviously cause the bar to be moved (think stroke tempo) much more slowly than at lighter loads. I believe the same concept applies to Pure Power, maximum-strength work in the pool, and to fully train the neuromuscular system and to move toward absolute maximum strength, we must challenge our swimmers with maximal or near-maximal loads that, yes, will cause them to stroke with a tempo that is slower than true race pace. While they may not be hitting race-pace tempo on heavy Power Tower loads, if the intent to move is at a maximum effort and the load is heavy, they will elicit maximum strength gains.

The question then becomes, does a maximal strength gain elicited by Pure Power training with a slower tempo, in an extremely similar stroking pattern to untethered free swimming, have any carryover to said swimming at true race tempo? Some coaches will disagree, but I do believe there certainly is carryover, though I cannot prove it scientifically.

There are several prominent coaches who take issue with the lack of hitting true race-pace tempo, and I certainly respect their right to disagree. I raise this thought, however—isn't it funny that some of the same coaches who shun Pure Power resistance training at maximal loads because it does not allow athletes to hit race-pace tempo are perfectly fine with prescribing repeat 800s where, surprise, athletes are also not hitting true race-pace tempo? Are said coaches concerned about race-pace tempo across the board, or do they single out Pure Power-type work because it features 12.5s and heavy resistance on "toys" and not repeat 400s?

I submit to you that if a coach believes that stroking below true race-pace tempo on a Power Tower is detrimental, said coach had better feel the same about a T3000. And if such is the case, then USRPT is the only way our hypothetical coach could possibly train, as all strokes in true USRPT are at specific race tempo. And we all know how USRPT is viewed at the highest levels of our sport; race-pace training is a piece of the pie, yes, but should not be the only piece, with the overwhelming majority of top-level coaches in agreement that a holistic approach is best.

Sample Sets

I will list a number of Pure Power sets, some of which I created specifically for this book and have not used in workouts, but the majority of sets will be from actual workouts at Arizona, Penn State, and Liberty. I will list the location of each set and the coach who authored said workout. I am thankful that Bill Dorenkott inspired me to adopt the habit of recording all workouts while at PSU, and it has been a habit that has stuck with me over the years. I recorded all of our workouts over the years (SCY and LCM) here at Liberty, and I have taken the practice one step further by recording my thoughts about each workout after the fact; I list what worked, what did not, the results or times from the workout, what could be done better in the future, and so forth.

Speaking of recording workouts, while at Arizona I recorded all of Rick DeMont's sprint workouts, my thoughts, the thoughts of the UA staff, and any other interesting notes into an unpublished book aptly named *A Tucson Summer*, and often refer back to those workouts for inspiration and a creative spark. Hopefully, Rick DeMont's success as a sprint coach needs no introduction to the readers of this book, and I cannot state enough how grateful I am to have had the opportunity to learn from one of the giants in our sport. To have an entire long-course season of

DeMont workouts (with his infamous quotes) at my fingertips is a pleasure, to say the least.

Again, the three basics of our Pure Power training here at Liberty are simple: short blast efforts of 12.5 yards or 15 meters, all-out maximal efforts (Hammer Down as Sam Freas would say), and heavy bucket loads with plenty of rest, the load relative, again, to the level of development of the individual athlete.

With those three guidelines, the possibilities are endless in terms of the creative process and what our collective cognitive genius, as a body of coaches, can produce. In no way do I believe we have the absolute best Pure Power sets or thought processes here at Liberty, and I am sure there are coaches out there doing it better—though I may or may not speak differently to recruits! The following are simply examples of what has worked and does work for us, and it is your job as a critical thinker and cerebral coach to take what you will read here, examine it, attack it from all angles, experiment with it, and find what works for you, your program, and your athletes. For the following examples, assume all efforts are on no time interval, unless otherwise noted.

University of Arizona
Wednesday June 20, 2007
Sprint Group Power
Written by Rick DeMont

Six Rounds:

All efforts MAX

Rounds 1-2 = No Gear

Rounds 3-4 = Fins

Rounds 5-6 = Fins + Paddles

1 X 20 Bucket Full

1 X 20 Bucket filled 2/3

1 X 20 Bucket filled 1/3

1 X 20 No Bucket

This set was a pleasure to watch, as you could see the pop in the stroke increase as the bucket weight decreased. Rick prescribed similar progressions quite often at Arizona, and perhaps without knowing it, he was indeed tapping into the Post-Activation Potentiation effect I will discuss at length in Chapter Seven. The last 20-yard effort with no bucket was fast, and a PAP effect from the full bucket was certainly at play for the 2/3 and 1/3 loads as well.

University of Arizona
Friday June 8, 2007
Sprint Group Power
Written by Rick DeMont

8 X 15 Power Tower Full Bucket

O = Kick with fins

E = Swim with fins + paddles

Sometimes keeping it simple is best, and Rick would often give the Arizona sprint group a basic Tower set consisting of kick and swim efforts, such as the one above. No frills, no gimmicks, just 8 X 15s as fast as you can go, focusing on maxing out the underwater body dolphin on the kick and hitting an efficient early vertical forearm and high elbow with a "big" stroke on the swim efforts.

Made Up for the Book

Six Rounds:

3 X 12.5 Max Blast Swim on the Power Tower @ 1:15 with fins, paddles, snorkel, bucket filled 50% on rounds 1-2, 75% on rounds 3-4, and 100% on rounds 5-6

1 X 50 EZ Swim between rounds

Post-Activation Potentiation Variation:*

Six Rounds:

3 X 12.5 Max Blast Swim @ 1:15 with fins, paddles, snorkel, bucket filled 50% on rounds 1-2, 75% on rounds 3-4, and 100% on rounds 5-6

1 X 15 Max Blast Swim after each 3 X 12.5, no Power Tower, odd rounds from a push with choice of gear, even rounds from a dive, choice flat or relay start

*Again, I will speak at length on PAP in Chapter Seven. If you are looking for super-fast swimming, this is the way to go!

Liberty University
Wednesday June 8, 2016
Team Power
Written by Jake Shellenberger

Four Rounds:

2 X 12.5 Max Blast Swim heavy Power Tower

2 X 12.5 Max Blast Swim heavy Power Tower + heavy weight belt

2 X 15 Dive Max with heavy weight belt flat or relay

1 X 15 Dive Max flat or relay

This is a classic Post-Activation Potentiation set, and I give our sprint group a heavy dose of PAP work during nearly every Pure Power workout here at Liberty—all season long, not just during a taper. This type of progression leads to ultra-fast dive times, and as I will explain in Chapter Seven, the times we hit on the dive 15s are faster than had we not prescribed the Pure Power work beforehand. The Towers and weight belts "light up" and "switch on" the neuromuscular system, readying the body for faster-than-normal performances.

Liberty University
Friday May 20, 2016
Mid + Distance Group Power
Written by Assistant Coach Jessica Barnes

Four Rounds:

Jake Shellenberger

2 X 12.5 Max Blast Swim heavy Power Tower with fins + tennis balls

2 X 12.5 Max Blast Swim heavy Power Tower with fins + paddles

1 X 25 Max Blast Swim, push, with heavy weight belt + choice of gear

1 X 25 Dive Max, flat or relay start, no gear

We sprint often with tennis balls, the goal being to take away the hand and to "switch on" any sensory receptors that might be asleep in the forearms. This type of work is excellent for teaching feel for the water at maximum velocity, and I will cover more in Chapter Five on drilling with resistance.

Liberty University
Friday May 20, 2016
Sprint Group Power
Written by Jake Shellenberger

Five Rounds:

3 X 12.5 Max Blast Swim, heavy Power Tower with choice of gear

1 X 15 Dive Max, flat start, with heavy weight belt

1 X 25 Dive Max, flat start, to a foot touch

This set produced an 11.1 effort on the 25 to a foot touch from a 22.9 freestyler. Now, yes, my watch might be a bit quick, and we should add another tenth or two if the feet were to activate the pad on a real foot-touch effort, but I will certainly take any effort in the 11-point-low range. This type of progression will elicit fast swimming!

Liberty University
July 1, 2016
Sprint Group Power
Written by Jake Shellenberger

Four Rounds:

3 X 12.5 Max Blast Swim, bucket filled 3/4 to full

1 X 25 Dive Max from a relay start to a foot touch

This set produced several 10.6 and 10.7 efforts on the 25, and we love to see anything in the mid-10-second range as my stat keeping over the years has shown we have a good chance of splitting 22.5 or better at our conference meet if we can consistently hit 10.6 in season.

Liberty University
April 9, 2012
Sprint Group Power
Written by Jake Shellenberger

Five Rounds:

3 X 12.5 Max Blast Swim, bucket filled 3/4 to full, with fins

    1 = Tennis Balls

    2 = No Paddles

    3 = Largest Paddles

1 X 12.5 Max Blast Swim from a whistle float on the Power Tower with fins and choice of paddles

1 X 15 Max Blast Swim no Power Tower

Again, we saw many fast efforts on the final 15, and the float sprinting from a whistle start on the Tower forced the athletes to recruit as many muscle fibers and motor units as possible and to do so as quickly as possible. I will discuss float sprinting in more detail in Chapter Nine.

Liberty University
1RM Test and Warmup
Sprint Group Power
Written by Jake Shellenberger

One Round:

3 X 12.5 Swim @ 80% effort on the Power Tower with bucket filled 1/2, with choice of gear

2 X 12.5 Swim @ 90% effort on the Power Tower with bucket filled 3/4, with choice of gear

1 X 12.5 Max Blast Swim on the Power Tower with full bucket, with choice of gear

1 X 12.5 Max Blast Swim on the Power Tower with new max record attempt

1 X 12.5 Max Blast Swim on the Power Tower with new max record attempt

Etc.

The above set is an example of how we approach a 1RM Power Tower attempt. This set always follows a lengthy warm-up, with a good amount of pulling to make sure the shoulders are loose. The athletes keep adding water and/or weight until they can no longer complete the 12.5-yard effort. This set is always a blast for our women, and we turn the music up to full volume and tell them to explore what inner aggression they can summon. "Tsunami" by DVBBS & Borgeous is a favorite track, and when it drops, if you can time a 12.5-yard max attempt to the bass when it hits, you are going to see some great efforts!

Chapter 4: Power Endurance

"A lot of people run a race to see who is the fastest. I run to see who has the most guts, who can punish himself into exhausting pace, and then at the end, push himself even more."

Steve Prefontaine

THERE IS a quote in swimming circles in regards to NASCAR and the concept of lap money, specifically the lack thereof in our sport, and how it matters not who is first at the first wall, no, our sport is all about who is first at the last wall. As such, Power Endurance in the general sense is the name of the game, and every coach should be looking to elicit maximum power output in the stroke applied to the water for the entirety of the specific race distance. Call it speed endurance, anaerobic power endurance, or aerobic power endurance for the distance types; the goal is maximum power output throughout the three energy systems over the length of the race—power endurance in the general sense, if you will.

As this book is not meant to delve too deeply into the physiology of our sport, I will not go into the ATP-CP, anaerobic, or aerobic energy systems in great detail, but I will highlight how Power Endurance training on the Power Tower can improve capacity and why I believe that Power Endurance is of supreme importance for all events. Even with the SCY 50 free, when considering the number of strokes taken, the rep ranges, if you will, (when compared to the weight room) mirror the endurance end of said ranges and not maximum strength, and this is certainly the case in the long course 50. Consider the following examples of how Power Endurance is key for even our shortest race:

Prior to this year, the NCAA record in the 50-yard freestyle was held by Arizona's Lara Jackson, set while leading off the Wildcats 200 freestyle relay at NCAAs in 2009. Even with fantastic underwaters, Jackson took twelve strokes down and fifteen back, and twenty-seven repetitions of anything is an endurance event, not a feat of one-rep maximum strength.

Likewise at NCAAs in 2015, Simone Manuel of Stanford was out in fourteen strokes and home in fifteen for twenty-nine total on her way to a blistering 21.32 time. Olivia Smoliga, who set the NCAA record of 21.21 at this year's NCAA championships, was down in approximately twelve strokes and back in approximately thirteen, again twenty-five strokes total being a feat of Power Endurance, not a one-repetition maximum.

Is the combination of Power Endurance and the endurance/reserve capacity of the ATP-CP and early anaerobic system important in the 50? It certainly is! Consider that in 2015 Manuel was third to the wall but was home an incredible 10.82 to win the event by nearly three-tenths of a second. Maximum power output over twenty-nine strokes is indeed a matter of Power Endurance, and the longer the ATP-CP system can provide maximum contractile force, the faster one can finish even our shortest race. That is to say, oftentimes even the 50 will go to the athlete who has trained their ATP-CP system to hold on longer, not to the athlete who has maxed out the first eight to ten seconds of ATP-CP production.

Of the thirteen individual events in the NCAA format, ten are distances of 200 yards and less, and when one considers the five relays, fifteen of eighteen events in the college program are 200-and-under events, seventy-six percent and eighty-three percent, respectively. If a coach were to focus then, it would make sense to focus on the events that are 200 yards and less, and Power Endurance work on the Power Tower is fantastic for developing specific anaerobic power endurance as it relates to muscular endurance over the course of a 200-and-under distance.

Our entire team here at Liberty engages in some form of Power Endurance work at least twice a week, with our mid-distance and distance groups, of course, engaging in the majority of our Power Endurance, focusing on the 100/200 for stroke types and the 200/500/1650 for freestyle types.

I define Power Endurance in broader terms than Pure Power, as one can turn any distance and nearly any bucket load into a Power Endurance-focused set. Consider the 12.5-yard or 15-meter distances of Pure Power, for example; it is entirely possible to turn 12.5s into a great Power Endurance workout by simply lowering the rest interval and the load of the bucket. Efforts may or may not be sub-maximal, depending on the set, and the rest interval will also vary depending on the goal of the set. As with Pure Power, we may or may not hit race-specific tempo, and, again, I believe there is absolutely a carryover to free, untethered racing, even without hitting said race-specific tempo.

As such, here at Liberty, our Power Endurance work consists of the following guidelines:

1. 12.5-yard or 15-meter repeat efforts with a load comparable to 40-60% of a 1RM max bucket effort with a short rest interval

2. 25-yard repeat distances with a 30-50% load, with a short-to-medium rest interval

3. 100-200 repeat distances* or more with a 30% load and a short-to-medium rest interval (I should note some of our advanced athletes can hit the 50% load mark for 100-200 repeat distances, however this is rare.)

*At Arizona, Penn State, and here at Liberty, when we prescribe(d) 100s, 150s, 200s and so forth on the Tower in a specific way, we are speaking directly to the resisted 25 effort, not the entire swim. For example, we might go a Power Endurance set of:

6 X 100 @ 2:00 on the Power Tower, 95%, 100% by P.T. 25

By "P.T. 25" we refer to the resisted 25-yard efforts. The even 25s are moderate-pace backstroke, letting the bucket pull the athlete back along the way. We never go full 100s max on the Tower. To decrease the amount of rest, we simply instruct the athletes to swim backstroke a bit faster; again we never go full 100s max on the Tower with turns and so forth.

In short, Power Endurance work on the Power Tower would compare well to circuit-training, power-endurance, or general muscular-endurance work in the weight room, featuring lower weight, higher work and repetition ranges, and a shorter rest interval. As this type of work is not nearly as taxing on the neuromuscular system as Pure Power, the athletes can handle a much higher volume, and a higher volume is obviously important for training the 200-and-longer race distances, specifically.

From an in-water physiological standpoint, Power Endurance work matches up quite well with the anaerobic work we see in race-pace training, and we might consider this kind of work lactate-tolerance work if comparing it to an untethered swimming set. The goals include increasing

Jake Shellenberger

muscular endurance, increasing the pain threshold of the athlete, and increasing anaerobic power and capacity.

Power Endurance Season Planning Considerations

Short Course (September to March)

As with Pure Power, we start our Power Endurance work with our mid-distance group in October every year, and as with Pure Power, we have started as early as September with our older, more advanced athletes in the past and will continue to do so in the future. It is with Power Endurance where we break with the classic Bompa periodization protocol, as he would advise building a certain level of maximum strength before transitioning to true Power Endurance. While our mid-distance and distance types do engage in Pure Power, maximum-strength work all year, the majority of their focus is on Power Endurance, starting in October and continuing to our conference meet in February.

In contrast to Pure Power, we are quick to begin freshmen and sophomores on Power Endurance training, as the loads are much lower. It is not uncommon, for example, for freshmen to go the same distance in a Power Endurance set as juniors or seniors, albeit with a lighter load. Again, as with Pure Power, this is highly individualized, and 500/1650 types will go different Power Endurance sets than 100/200-stroke types and certainly different sets than sprint freestyle types.

We tend not to measure Power Endurance work primarily by bucket load as with Pure Power, instead focusing on weekly volume, starting out in the 500-yard range and building up to 2000 yards or more by the end of January, before tapering off for the conference meet. We follow the same three-week rest protocol, and it is amazing to see the "pop" in the stroke when the mid-distance and distance types start to drop the volume and bucket load during the three weeks of taper. While, again, Power Endurance work is not as taxing on the neuromuscular system as is Pure Power, the supercompensation effect is still rather large, and our 200/500 time-drops at our conference meet are significant, certainly comparable to the relay drops I listed previously. Consider three examples, specifically:

Our 500-freestyle school record is 4:48.87, set in 2014, and that same athlete had a best in-season time that year of 5:02.05. Our school record in the 200 fly, also set in 2014, saw a drop from a best in-season time of 2:02.84 to 1:56.79—an NCAA-qualifying swim at our conference meet. Our 200-breast school record, again set in 2014, this time at NCAAs, is 2:11.99, down from a 2:16.68 best in-season time.

Power Endurance Season Planning Considerations

Long Course (April - July/August)

Ah yes, long course meters. Contrary to popular belief, my favorite swimming event is not the 50 free SCY, nor the SCY 200 free relay or SCY 200 medley. No, my favorite race is the LCM 50 free, and my favorite relay is the LCM 4x100 freestyle. The LCM 50 free is as pure as it gets in our sport, in my humble opinion, of course. Walk through it with me . . . one lap, no turns, all-out max from start to finish, the race going to the athlete who can combine that perfect blend of top-end speed and speed endurance. The race is won from the 25-meter mark to the wall, and it is in those final 25 meters where Power Endurance makes all the difference, combined, of course, with a finish of the finest technical excellence. The big pool, as they say, separates the men from the boys and the women from the girls, and Power Endurance is what separates Olympic gold from obscurity, and many times the difference is less than a tenth of a second.

Quoting Rick DeMont, once again, I had the chance to talk to him at summer nationals in 2009, after Lara Jackson set her aforementioned then-American and NCAA record that winter in the 50 free, and after congratulating him on the swim, he replied, "Yeah, it was awesome, but now I need to teach her how to swim."

This was in reference, of course, to the transfer of that SCY speed to the LCM format and the different skill set that the LCM 50 free requires. But imagine that—his athlete just swam the fastest 50-yard freestyle in history, and his focus was on "teach[ing] her how to swim" in the big pool.

We max out our Power Endurance volume in the summer long course season with our sprint and mid-distance groups here at Liberty, and the overwhelming majority of the mid-distance group's Power Tower work has a Power Endurance focus in the summer, with little work in the Pure Power range. Our sprint group also focuses more on Power Endurance in the summer than during the SCY season, but they still do quite heavy, if not their heaviest, Pure Power work in the summer as well. Similar to the SCY season, we measure Power Endurance by total volume during the summer, and we will max out at nearly 3,000 yards' worth in our highest peak week in late June.

Recovery Considerations

Again, I believe that, because Power Endurance is not nearly as taxing on the neuromuscular system as is Pure Power, our women can handle a higher volume with less recovery than with true Pure Power work. Humans have an incredible capacity for endurance, certainly much more so than for maximum strength and pure power. While a thousand-plus-pound deadlift as a measure of raw, 1RM-strength is impressive, the 100-mile-ultramarathon world record is far more impressive, in my humble opinion, and I admit to as much coming from a power/strength background, believing in a low-volume, high-intensity approach to training, and being a self-proclaimed "sprint coach." While I have a heart for speed and power, I must give endurance athletes credit where credit is due.

At the time of this writing, said 100-mile record is held by Russian Oleg Kharitonov, at 11:28.03, or an average of 6:53 per mile over 100 miles. This record is mind-boggling, and when we think of some of the great distance swimming sets of all time and the sheer volume that many of our distance swimmers log in the pool, we see that our bodies are certainly built more for endurance than for raw speed, power, and strength.

We keep the same Thursday recovery day in our LCM schedule, and this has worked well for us over the years, even with a higher overall summer volume for both our sprint and mid-distance groups. As with Pure Power work during the LCM season, because stress levels are lower compared to the school year, we train outside in a LCM pool, and the sun is shining, we feel as though our women can and certainly do handle a higher volume in the summer with the same amount of recovery. In short, while recovery should be a focus at all times, for both short and long course, feel free to work at a higher volume with Power Endurance, especially during the summer LCM season.

Taper Considerations

We follow the same taper protocol during the college season for Power Endurance work that we implement for Pure Power, reaching our highest-volume week in middle-to-late January, followed by our three-week taper heading into the conference meet. The reductions of volume and load also mirror that of Pure Power, and we have found that a 50% and then 33% reduction of the volume each week leaves our 100/200 stroke and IM types in great physical and psychological shape heading into the third week of taper and into our conference meet. Our 200/500/1650 types tend to stay a bit higher with their Power Endurance volume during the taper, but again, this is highly individualized, as it could be that a 200-fly type also wants to higher.

Power Endurance General Thoughts

For the same reasons mentioned in the previous chapter on Pure Power, I am once again of the belief that this type of work does not always need to be performed at specific race tempo. Again, if we compare Power Endurance to "free swimming" lactate-tolerance work, we see specific anaerobic changes in the body still taking place, even at slower-than-race-pace tempo. Certainly the number of coaches are few who would shut down a race-pace set on the last round with three efforts to go because the athletes were no longer hitting specific race-pace tempo. Why then, must we shut down a Power Endurance set for the same reasons?

Similarly, if we were working a true endurance set in the weight room or in dryland—perhaps three rounds of 30 reps of a circuit or 60 seconds on and 20 off for several rounds of med ball throws and so forth—certainly the lift tempo and med-ball-throw tempo would slow by the end of each round and certainly by the end of the circuit. I would guess that the majority of coaches, however, would be fine with letting the circuit continue—I do believe we instinctively know that beneficial training adaptations are taking place, even if the tempo has slowed.

Back to a pool example and a final point I would like to make in regards to specific race-pace tempo and power training in general: suppose we did limit athletes who could no longer hit specific race tempo, shutting them down the minute they fell off true race pace, whether it be on Power Towers, USRPT, or dive lactate tolerance . . . if these athletes are never offered the chance to push through that point of falling off race-pace tempo in practice, how do we expect them to push past the same point in a race? I do not believe that failure in practice is a bad thing. Let us fail and die in practice to succeed and live in a race!

Power Endurance work can be extremely painful, and only the bravest of athletes will truly get up and give it their all during this type of training. Lactate tolerance "free swimming" is painful . . . lactate-tolerance work with resistance is certainly more so! Anyone who has gone beyond failure in the weight room or who has subjected themselves to the infamous "burnout" sets can attest that when you add resistance to lactate-tolerance work, the game changes drastically.

Arizona engaged in quite a bit of Power Endurance-type work during my time there in 2007, and looking back it is no surprise they have, and continue, to excel in the mid-distance events. Not only is this type of work great for the back end of a 200, it allows for some great easy speed going out when combined with Pure Power, which the Arizona mid-distance types did quite well.

Power Endurance Example Sets

University of Arizona
May 23, 2007
Whole Team Power
Written by Frank Busch

10 X 100 @ 2:30 Max Swim, Power Tower, with fins and paddles, various bucket loads

Again, the even 25s were swim backstroke at a moderate pace, letting the Tower pull them back to the wall.

Penn State University
Annual Sprint Group Power Tower Challenge Set
2007-2009
Written by Bill Dorenkott

6 X 300 Max Blast Swim, no time interval, with fins, paddles, and snorkel, with a heavy bucket relative to the athlete's strength, general ability, and number of years in the program

This was a test set we implemented at PSU, inspired by Arizona, with a bit of a Randy Reese influence as well. Distance swimmers have their legendary test sets and mental-challenge sets, and this was our version for the sprint group at PSU. This set was more a test of the mind than anything else, though I have to believe it also helped us finish a 200.

Liberty University
May 16, 2016
Mid/Distance Group Power
Written by Jessica Barnes

Three Rounds:

4 X 50 @ 1:10 Max Blast Swim with weight belt on the Power Tower, medium bucket

2 X 150 @ 2:30 Max Blast Swim with no weight belt on the Power Tower

100 Easy

Liberty University
May 30, 2016
Mid/Distance Group Power
Written by Jessica Barnes

Four Rounds:

1 X 150 @ 3:00 Max Blast Swim with weight belt on the Power Tower, medium bucket

4 X 15 @ :30 Max Blast Swim with no weight belt on the Power Tower, medium bucket

Jake Shellenberger

100 Easy

*1 X 50 Push Max for time after round four

This set produced quite a few fast efforts on the 50 push from our mid and distance types, and my guess is that a bit of Post-Activation Potentiation was present, along with the Power Endurance focus.

Liberty University
May 28, 2016
Sprint Group Power
Written by Jake Shellenberger

Six Rounds:

12 X 10 @ :20 Max Blast Swim on the Power Tower, bucket filled 1/3, with choice of paddles, no fins

Extra 10 seconds rest, paddles off

2 X 25 @ :20 Push Max, goal is 11 seconds for the 25-yard effort and 8.4 seconds for the final 15 meters, timed from the head at the 15-meter mark to the finish at the wall.

This was a fantastic set and did, in fact, produce a few swims in the 11-second range from two of our best sprinters, with the fastest at 11.6. Though we did not hit the 8.4-second goal for 15 meters, we were close, with quite a few efforts below 9 seconds with our fastest at 8.60. As for the 8.4-second goal, we use the Australian speed charts for our LCM training here at Liberty, and the charts tell us if a goal is 25.8 in the LCM 50 freestyle, we should try to hit a goal time of 8.4 in training for the final 15 meters of the swim, timed from the head at the 35-meter mark to the finish at the wall.

As I believe the 50 free LCM is won from the 25 and, in many cases, the 35-meter mark to the wall, our goal with this set was to put the body in a physiological state that mirrors the 35-meter mark in a race. As for SCY, if we can come home anywhere close to eleven point mid we are going twenty-two point plus in the 50, as getting out eleven point low to the turn is something we do well here at Liberty.

48

Jake Shellenberger

Liberty University
May 11, 2016
Sprint Group Power
Written by Jake Shellenberger

Six Rounds:

4 X 50 @ 1:00 Descend 1-2, 3-4 by P.T. 25 to Max with a medium-weight bucket

4 X 25 @ :30 Descend 1-2, 3-4 to Max with heavy weight belt, no Tower

2 X 50 @ :50 Tight Descend 1-2 to *fast* but not Max

This type of set is fantastic for 50/100 types that go up to the 200, as the Power Tower and weight belt work train the early anaerobic and late ATP-CP system for Power Endurance, and the 50 *fast* but not max at the end teaches the athletes to swim fast without muscle, fast but controlled, and to do so in a fatigued state. By tight descend, we wouldn't want the first 50 to be an EZ float with the second 50 fast. For example, we would ask a sub-1:50.00 200-freestyle sprinter to go 29 and then 27 seconds for the 50s with a perceived effort of 80% and then 93%, and if we can hit 27 on a set such as this one, we know that we have a good shot to bring our 200s home in 27+ at our conference meet.

Oftentimes it is a challenge for pure sprint types who know two speeds, max and easy, to swim fast while controlled, and this phenomenon is certainly evident to the many coaches who have seen their pure sprinters fail to hold on to the end of the 200 free. This set can help!

In closing, Power Endurance separates the elite from the great and the great from the good, and, again, every coach should be looking to maximize power output over the target number of stroke cycles in a given race. Endurance training on the Towers can help tremendously, and this should be a high focus priority for all events, as again, I believe even the 50 free is a race decided by Power Endurance.

Chapter 5: Drilling

"That looks so good."

Me

"I know, I love watching it. I learn from it. The teachers are in the pool."

Rick

Rick DeMont and myself talking about Roland Schoeman's stroke and his impeccable attention to detail while drilling. June 4, 2007 Tucson, Arizona

WHILE CERTAINLY Pure Power and Power Endurance work are the most popular forms of Power Tower training, I decided to dedicate an entire chapter of this book to drilling and other forms of "slow swimming" on resistance for two reasons. One, while it may not be the most popular or the most fun form of resistance training for our athletes, like Tom Meade, I believe it is immensely beneficial for their stroke development and technical efficiency in general. Two, I believe that drilling and other forms of slow swimming (henceforth referred to as tech swimming) are fantastic for inclusion as a part of a main set, similar to how we use Post-Activation Potentiation, which I will discuss in Chapter Seven.

There are a few coaches in our sport, mainly those from the "USRPT only" school of thought, who do not believe that drilling or slow swimming with a tech focus of any kind has a place in the training of elite athletes. As I am dedicating an entire chapter to resisted drilling, I respectfully disagree. I believe that healthy debate is good for our sport in general, and I aim to give powerful reasons in this chapter as to why resisted drilling at well below race pace is beneficial for our athletes and should be a part of every swimmer's training, especially sprint types.

As you will see from the sample sets, drilling and tech swimming on the Power Tower is quite similar to Power Endurance work, and early-season drilling with resistance doubles as Power Endurance work for our sprint crew here at Liberty. Many of the sets are similar, and a Power Endurance set can become a drill set quite easily with a change in gear and bucket weight. One could also combine the two styles of training, and I will out-line in this chapter several ways in which we do just that. We do not have a specific definition of tech or drill work on the Towers, but I will mention a few loose rules that we follow.

Drilling and tech work against resistance, here at Liberty, for all of our athletes involves mostly sub-maximal efforts, with an extremely light bucket, with the goal of improving stroke technique and feel for the water. Our women are instructed to focus deliberately on their strokes, using this type of training as a meditation of sorts, with a keen awareness of their bodies in space and what helps them to go faster and to move through the water more efficiently. I believe this "play" time and period of self-awareness is beneficial to those who truly embrace it, and our goal is to move all of our women to a point at which they become master techni-cians, to the point where they know their strokes inside and out, better even than we as coaches. The ultimate goal is that eventually our athletes can tell us where they lacked efficiency in a race or set and that they can tell us where their technique broke down or went awry, and perhaps most importantly, they can tell us how they might go about fixing the ineffi-ciencies.

This is a definite challenge, as some of our athletes (and yours) default to simply going through the motions and mindlessly swimming through drilling sets, whether on resistance or not. We have some tips and tricks that we use to nudge our women in the direction of focusing intently on their technique, but the reality of this training is that the athletes must simply embrace it fully, with 100% of their focus and dedication commit-ted to the tasks at hand. This "living in the now" mentality is hard for many to grasp, in swimming and in life in general. Many live in the past and in the future, while few are intently living in the now, fully focused on the present. If you are familiar with Phil Jackson's coaching philoso-phy, this is the "zen" part of swim training, and again I do believe it is beneficial to those who embrace it fully.

As Rick stated, "The teachers are in the pool," This went far beyond the immense talent and skill level of the Arizona team of 2007, for Frank and Rick truly steered that team to the point of the technical mastery I previ-ously mentioned. It was not Rick who was the world's foremost expert on Lara Jackson's technique (he was a close second), nor was it Frank who was the world's foremost expert on Lacey Nymeyer's technique (again, a close second). No, it was Lara and Lacey who were the number-one expert technicians of their own strokes, and they in fact taught their coaching staff where, when, and how their technique broke down in training and in races. Rick said about Courtney Cashion, "She knows right where that stuff is that makes her go faster." Yes, she had one of the best early vertical forearm positions I had ever seen up until that point in my coaching career.

That summer, I witnessed many examples firsthand of the Arizona athletes truly embracing the now, focusing intensely on their technique, and truly becoming masters of their own strokes. For anyone who doubts the above, consider that it simply must have been true; the next school year both the Arizona men and women won NCAA Division I team titles, a feat only possible when the majority, perhaps an overwhelming majority, of a team is bought into the "now" and indeed becomes masters of their own techniques. That kind of elite-level dominance simply cannot happen any other way.

In regards to our resisted tech work here at Liberty, we are specifically looking for three characteristics of technique with our drilling on resistance.

First and perhaps foremost, we are looking to hone the classic early vertical forearm, a position sought by many in our sport and achieved by few. This hallmark of technical excellence is important for all freestyle and fly types, but I do believe it is especially important for the sprint freestyle races. There simply is not enough time to "lay out" on the front end of the stroke with a low or even horizontal elbow, as sprint free types must get to the catch and achieve the early vertical forearm (henceforth EVF) quickly in the stroke.

Watch any men's or women's 50-freestyle Olympic final since 2000 on YouTube to see the EVF in action, or go even farther back to the Matt Biondi versus Tom Jager match race from 1990 to see an example of "old school" EVF on display. Simply type "Biondi vs. Jager" into YouTube or type this link into your browser:

https://youtu.be/AMT-vPMAoIA

Jake Shellenberger

It is quite impressive to watch Jager go 21.81 in a brief, with a lot of hair, and with no track plate on the block. While Biondi and Jager did not incorporate a "straight arm" recovery, they do both get to the catch quickly and waste no time laying out on the water with a horizontal elbow. I do wonder how fast they could have been with a straighter arm recovery—both were quite short with their strokes and would have taken fewer strokes with a longer recovery.

A side note on sprint technique: We do teach a straight(er) arm recovery for our sprint types here at Liberty, and Mike Bottom fans will know this as the shoulder-driven freestyle. I believe this is the fastest way to swim sprint free, and I believe we should attempt to attach as much strength and power to the longest levers possible. This length is only possible with a straight-arm recovery. We do not want any forward movement of the hand or arm after they enter the water, therefore we must achieve the length on the recovery. See Florent Manaudou's or Abbey Weitzeil's techniques as two prime examples. Regarding Manaudou specifically, in my humble opinion, his 50-free gold from London is perhaps the best display of sprint freestyle technique our sport has ever produced; know that I write these words pre-Rio.

Second, we are looking to increase distance per stroke with our resistance drill work and tech swimming, and we feature quite a few drills that are fantastic for doing so. Finally, we attempt to "increase" or "make better," if you will, the feel of the water, a phenomenon that is certainly crucial to elite-level swimming.

Feel for the water is a fascinating aspect of technical excellence, as it is hard to describe, but every coach knows it when they see it. There are many coaches who believe that feel is innate, that it is part of the talent of our sport, and that it cannot be taught. I disagree in part and subscribe more to the Anders Ericsson 10,000-hours concept found in his latest book, "Peak," which, paraphrasing, says that the characteristics of greatness that we see in elite athletes and often label as talent are nothing more than the outcome of a large amount of deliberate practice over the course of many years.

I do believe that feel for the water can be taught, improved, and that the brain can in fact "learn to feel more water," for lack of a better term. I believe in the concept of neuroplasticity, and I believe that, yes, we can make changes to the brain over time that were once thought to be innate—talent, if you will. Here at Liberty, our coaching philosophy is to recruit the most talented athletes we can (physically) then to celebrate hard work and deliberate practice once they arrive on campus; we do not celebrate talent in our program.

Not to get too far off track talking about talent, but having said as much, talent is certainly important, and I do not mean to overlook said importance or to downplay the physical characteristics that often define elite swimmers. I do believe in talent. Michael Phelps for example is 6'4" with a 6'7" or 6'8" wingspan. Matt Grevers and Yannick Agnel are both 6'8," while Florent Manaudou stands 6'6." That is talent, and in his book Ericsson concedes as much; there are physical limitations that prohibit some from excelling in a given sport. If you are a 5'5" male, for example, you will probably never play center in the NBA, regardless of how many hours of deliberate practice you put into the sport of basketball.

I believe feel for the water is a bit different in that I do believe it is something that can be learned and is coachable. If you have ever had the pleasure of coaching a synchronized swimmer-turned-pool athlete, you can understand where I am coming from, as they often have incredible feel for the water; I believe said feel was developed through long hours of sculling and learning to move their bodies in incredibly difficult positions with just their hands.

As mentioned, our drill and tech work on the Power Tower is characterized by the use of an extremely light bucket, and we believe resistance is extremely beneficial when drilling and focusing on tech swimming. As with Meade, I am a firm believer that technical inefficiencies are magnified with resistance Tower work, for if you are not moving forward, the Tower is either pulling you backwards or you are not moving whatsoever. The Tower then forces you to always be in the "moving forward" with regards to technique, and the brain learns, perhaps instinctively, at the subconscious level, where the dead spots occur in the stroke and can go about improving in those areas. This is also the case for Pure Power and Power Endurance work, though with the high stroke and kick rates achieved, I believe it is harder to consciously consider the inefficient parts of the stroke, as the athlete is more concerned with force production and with making the 12.5 than they are with focusing on any inefficiencies they may have.

Depending on the drill, the gear used, and the age and state of the pulleys on the Tower, oftentimes a coach need not fill the bucket with any water whatsoever to pinpoint exactly where an athlete may have technical flaws. The Power Tower can give a plethora of information to the coach with a keen eye toward technique; we need only look and listen to the Tower, and it will indeed teach us much.

I should note that the Power Tower is not the only piece of resistance equipment that can be used for drilling and other forms of tech swimming, and we use various resistance toys here at Liberty as a part of our resisted technique training. I will provide several examples of different resistance combinations that we use, and the possibilities are endless with regards to the creativity that can be unlocked and the results that can be achieved.

Another benefit to drilling and tech swimming with resistance is that many of the drill sets also double as "kick sets" in the sense that the athletes are forced to kick throughout the stroke if they want to maintain forward velocity. This type of work is fantastic for athletes who tend to "forget" to kick when they swim or for those who simply choose not to utilize their legs to the fullest potential. The resistance of the Power Tower and other toys will simply not let them get away with sloppy kick habits, and I will highlight a few examples in the sample sets.

Again, the possibilities are endless with regards to what coaches can dream up for drilling with resistance, and I certainly do not claim to have the best drills for Tower use. I will outline and highlight what works for us and why I believe in the drills we utilize, and I will also mention a few common drills that I believe are detrimental to sprint freestyle technique specifically, providing what I believe are powerful reasons why coaches should remove said drills from the training of their sprinters immediately.

Power Tower Drilling Sample Sets

Left/Right-Arm Swimming

As we know, balance in the stroke is crucial for success in our sport, perhaps nowhere more than in the sprint events—of all strokes. In the 50-yard freestyle for example, where a tiny mistake, or in this case a muscular strength imbalance, can determine the difference between an NCAA Champion and a runner-up, a difference of just 2% of power output in the left and right arms over the course of twenty-nine strokes can make or break the race. Consider the now-legendary Phelps versus Cavic 100-meter butterfly from Beijing in 2008 as the ultimate example—had Michael had a 1% greater difference in power output between left and right arms, we wouldn't be talking about eight golds. Phelps would certainly still be, without a doubt, the greatest of all-time, but an eight-time gold medal winner in a single Games he would not.

I believe the majority of our athletes have significant imbalances of strength and power between the right and left arms, and we can see this rather clearly in the weight room with dumbbell work. Ask an athlete to use heavy dumbbells for a given lift and you will see them struggling a bit more with the weaker arm. It is for this reason that we do a majority of our upper-body work with dumbbells, here at Liberty, and while this book is not meant to be a guide on strength training for swimming, I mention strength training here as it relates to limbs and strength/power imbalances in the pool. We do not bench press often, but when we do, it is with dumbbells, and many of our rows and overhead lifts are performed with dumbbells as we. Even cleans are occasionally done with dumbbells for the same reason—we want to make sure we are balanced from left to right as much as humanly possible, with the expectation that it will transfer to the pool.

Left/Right drilling on resistance, then, is one of many areas where we find that transfer to the pool, and it is a fantastic way to identify and to iron out any imbalances in the stroke, whether it be free, back, or fly. Breaststroke is a unique case when identifying limb imbalances, and we have a drill that gets close, which I will share. Arizona focused quite a bit on left/right swimming and the numerous variations, and did quite a bit of left/right work on the Towers as well. I took this training back to Penn

State the following school year, and it helped tremendously with Patrick Schirk's 200 backstroke. We had him train quite a bit of left/right backstroke on the Power Towers that year, and I am convinced that it was a major factor in his winning the NCAA title.

Left/Right work specifically does the following, among other benefits:

1. It teaches the brain/body balance in the stroke, not only in the left and right arms, but in the way they connect to the core and the legs.

2. It improves strength, power, and power endurance.

3. It improves the kick as a byproduct of the drill. Consider that on the recovery of the single arm, the only propulsion is provided by the legs. Quite often athletes will not work the kick as well as they should during regular, unresisted swimming, as the opposite arm is providing propulsion in freestyle and backstroke. In left/right swimming the legs must make up for the lack of propulsion of the opposite arm, forcing the athletes to kick through any dead spots they would normally have. It is the expectation, then, that with enough left/right work there will be a carryover to regular swimming, and they will continue to kick through said dead spots.

The creativity is endless with the types of sets one can prescribe here, and I will outline some of my favorites below.

"Arizona Style" Swimming

This is the famous left paddle/right fin drill, with the athletes switching between the opposites and then ending the set with fins and paddles. You may recognize this under a different name; I was first introduced to this drill at Arizona, and thus, in honor of the Wildcat program, call it "Zona Style" or simply "Zona" when writing workouts. This technique is fantastic for developing balance in the stroke and can be done as a drill, as a Power Endurance set, or as a Pure Power set, with the bucket load, rest prescribed, and set length determining which of the above goals the set will achieve. While Arizona Style is certainly more geared toward freestyle and backstroke types, we do use it for fly and breast, with the breaststroke types using paddles only, sans fins.

An example Arizona Style tech swimming on the Power Tower:

Three Rounds:

6 X 100 Arizona Style, with 1/3 or less bucket, at a tech focus pace, with choice of paddles

Arizona Style is always done in multiples of three, whether by effort or by round. As per the example above, you could go:

Three Rounds:

6 X 100 As

    2 X 100 With right paddle, left fin

    2 X 100 With left paddle, right fin

    2 X 100 With both fins and paddles

Or:

6 X 100 With right paddle, left fin

6 X 100 With left paddle, right fin

6 X 100 With both fins and paddles

Notes:

1. The athletes are instructed to focus on distance per stroke, taking the fewest possible number of strokes per 25. They will swim the "EZ" 25s recovery backstroke.

2. The athletes are instructed to count strokes. Ideally the stroke count on the left/right fin and paddle combinations are identical. If not, we know we have a stroke imbalance and can work to correct it.

3. The stroke count should be lower on the round with both paddles and both fins.

Jake Shellenberger

In a classic left/right drill set on the Tower, we might go similar to:

Three Rounds:

4 X 100 With Power Tower filled 1/3 bucket or less, with paddles and a snorkel for free and fly types, sans fins

100s 1-3 = 25 left arm / 25 EZ backstroke / 25 right arm / 25 EZ backstroke

100 #4 = Whole stroke, cruise, perhaps a pinch of speed

Notes:
1. In this basic left/right drill set we would want the athletes to count their strokes on the left/right 25s.
2. Ideally, they are taking the same number of strokes with each arm with the same stroke tempo.
3. Ideally, the speed of each left/right 25 is also the same. Again, we are looking for balance, with the same number of strokes, the same tempo, and the same time for each 25.
4. Our women feel incredible, for lack of a better term, on that fourth 100 when they put their full stroke together, and oftentimes they cannot help but open up the throttle a bit, as they feel that good in the water with the newfound balance in their strokes.

A variation of the above drill that, again, causes them to feel great in the water and produces some fast swimming in the process:

3 Rounds:

3 X 100 on the Power Tower, with choice of paddles if any, 1/3 bucket or less, going 25 left arm / 25 EZ backstroke / 25 right arm / 25 EZ backstroke, with a snorkel for free/fly types

Unhook Tower

50 swim at 85-93%, no gear, on a watch, focusing on great connectivity between the left and right arms, fast but not max swimming with no "muscle" in the stroke—fast and easy speed, if you will

Notes:
1. This variation leaves the athletes feeling balanced in the water.

2. We tend to see some *fast* efforts on the 50 with no Power Tower.

3. Perhaps best of all, the times we see on these efforts, while fast, are truly easy speed efforts, and we love to see the women going fast with no muscle, going fast without trying too hard to do so.

4. I believe there is immense value in learning how to swim super fast without going max, especially for 200 types, and in developing relaxed, easy front-end speed. Obviously, there are many ways to accomplish this goal, and we feel the above type of drill set on resistance is one of the best.

In yet another variation of the above set:

3 Rounds:

3 X 100 on the Power Tower, with anti-paddles, no fins, no water or a extremely small amount in the bucket, going 25 left arm / 25 EZ backstroke / 25 right arm / 25 EZ backstroke, with a snorkel for free/fly types

Unhook Tower with anti-paddles on—HANDS OUT, then take paddles off

50 swim at 85-93%, no gear, again focusing on great tech with easy speed—open it up a bit if you want!

Notes:

1. We use the Finis anti-paddles, however tennis balls will also work here if you do not have access to anti-paddles. If using tennis balls, pay careful attention to how the athletes are gripping the tennis balls in their hands—oftentimes they will get lazy and incorporate the palm or a few fingers into the stroke. The anti-paddles are best if you have them.

   The anti-paddles take the hand away, not allowing the brain to feel water on the hand and forcing it to "switch on" sensory receptors in the forearm to feel and ultimately "pull" more water.

   This helps the athlete to feel the EVF and to better grasp the concept of pulling water with the forearm.

2. By HANDS OUT, we mean rest on the wall with the hands completely out of the water. We instruct the women to not, under any circumstances, put their hands in the water until they push off the wall, not even a second before to scull or to get ready. We want them putting their hands in the water the absolute last moment before they push off the wall.

   The thought process here is that we want the last input the brain receives from the hand to be the feeling of no water with the anti-paddle. With the open hand, when the brain finally feels water again, it seems as though the athletes are pulling on concrete. While I don't know that the concept of "pulling more water" can be scientifically measured, if you watch closely on this drill you can actually see them pulling more water—distance per stroke has increased from the baseline prior to the anti-paddle work, and they simply "pull more water," for lack of a better term, after going from anti-paddle against resistance to an open hand and no resistance.

Again, an added benefit to left/right drilling on the Power Tower is the effect on the legs, as the athletes are forced to kick through dead periods in their recovery without their opposite arm to aid them. This effect is magnified immensely with the anti-paddles, as athletes are pulling much less water than they would with an open hand or with a training paddle. They must kick that much more to stay moving, and you can see the increased leg action on the 50 swim with no resistance, said action certainly aiding in the fast times that we see.

We prefer left/right work on the Power Towers for free, back, and fly types, and the three sets described here are just a few of the various ways one can drill or swim left/right. Breaststroke is a bit of a different animal, as single-arm breast on the Tower does not work well, and even if it did, I am not sure it would be productive. To work single arm for breaststroke we use a drill that Rick showed me at Arizona, named the "Yanko" drill, where the athlete either wears a buoy or kicks lightly, with the arms following the pattern:

1. Full breaststroke pull
2. Left arm breaststroke pull with opposite arm outstretched
3. Full breaststroke pull
4. Right arm breaststroke pull with the opposite arm outstretched
5. Repeat

The goal, as with the left/right drills, is to count the number of strokes and to reduce the count over time. This is also a great drill for fly types, and we use it often for our short-axis strokes.

Another drill—and its numerous variations—that we love for sprint freestyle types (and for everyone, for every stroke and every distance) is anything with the anti-paddles and the tennis balls I noted previously. The possibilities here are again endless, as any type of free swimming or drill on the Power Tower instantly becomes an EVF and brain-focused drill when the athletes wear the anti-paddles or tennis balls.

We swim regular stroke on the Towers with the anti-paddles. We also pull, scull, and train every other drill in our repertoire using these paddles. In my humble opinion, there is no better technique paddle than the anti-paddle, and we use it in some form in 90% of our training sessions here at Liberty, all year long. While, yes, the tennis balls serve a similar purpose, we do not drill with them often but instead save them for sprinting, as I believe that the anti-paddles are too heavy for sprint work. I have found over the past ten years of using tennis balls that athletes tend to "cheat" with them, as mentioned, and do not grip them deep enough in the palm to get a true anti-paddle effect. They often will grip them with just the thumb, index finger, and middle finger, leaving the rest of the hand open to feel and pull water.

As an example, while this is a great forearm position, as you can see the tennis ball resides between the thumb and the index finger, allowing the rest of the fingers and palm to feel water, defeating the purpose of the drill.

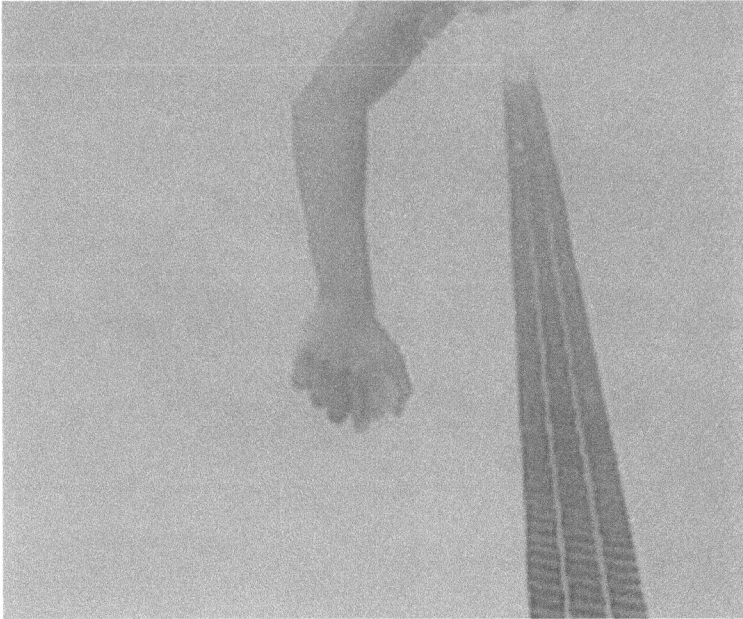

Sprinting with tennis balls, on the other hand, forces the athletes to use them correctly almost by default—at such high tempos the tennis balls will fall out unless they are gripped deep in the palm with the entire hand.

I have prescribed some form of anti-paddle work in nearly every workout over the past ten years at Penn State and Liberty, and I believe in them wholeheartedly. Again, the goal is to train the EVF and to teach the brain to involve sensory receptors in the forearms. Can we teach the brain to "feel" water on the forearm and to involve the forearm in the stroke? I believe—and the research that Anders Ericsson is producing at Florida State agrees—that yes we can! Here at Liberty, we teach that good athletes swim with their hands, great athletes swim with their hands and forearms, and elite athletes swim with their hands, forearms, and upper arms, even involving the bicep and triceps in the propulsive phase of the stroke. Again, we drill with the anti-paddles and sprint with the tennis balls, and I believe this type of drilling is extremely beneficial for all swimmers, in every event and every distance.

The Finis PT Paddles are our favorite anti-paddles, and while they are somewhat expensive, they are well worth the price, in my humble opinion. Again, there is no better technique paddle to teach the early vertical forearm and to train the brain to "feel" more water.

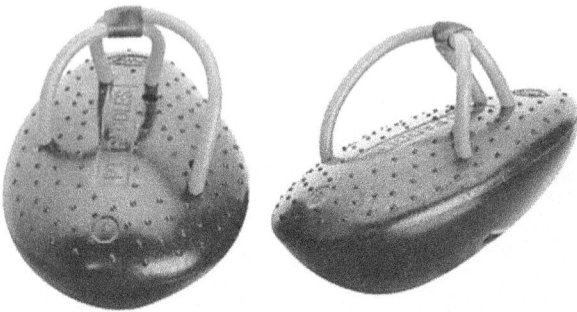

Anti-Paddle Example Sets

Three Rounds:

2 X 25 On the Power Tower with no water in the bucket, with anti-paddles, buoy, and snorkel, first 25 scull left arm only, second 25 scull right arm only

2 X 25 Scull with both arms, again on the Tower with the above gear

2 X 25 On the Tower, same gear, first 25 left arm pull, second 25 right arm pull

2 X 25 On the Tower, same gear, first 25 pull both arms at 75%, second 25 pull both arms at 85-93%

2 X 25 On the Tower, with anti-paddles, no buoy, with snorkel, first 25 swim left arm only, second 25 swim right arm only

2 X 25 On the Tower, with anti-paddles, no buoy, with snorkel, swimming full stroke, first 25 at 75%, second 25 at 85-93%

HANDS OUT

1 X 50 Swim, at 93%, with no gear

Note: This set takes quite a long time to complete, and you will have to weigh the benefits with the time costs. I believe in this type of work, and thus we take the time to do it. The volume is obviously quite low, just over 1000 yards, but I believe the benefit to the brain is worth 10,000 yards of low elbows and sloppy swimming.

This type of progression is beautiful to watch a highly skilled athlete attempt. For the lesser skilled, they will develop said skill with enough deliberate and focused practice, as they simply must to complete the set. Sculling with one arm, with an anti-paddle is hard; sculling with one arm, on a Power Tower, with an anti-paddle, even with no water in the bucket, is much harder still and is a highly advanced technique, indeed. This type of drill work will certainly separate the high-skill athletes from those without. However, I do believe that everyone can benefit, and everyone can learn much from this progression.

As with the left/right arm drills previously mentioned, the final 50 with no paddles or other gear often produces extremely fast times with little effort, as the brain has become accustomed to attempting to find propulsion with the forearm and pulls an incredible amount of water once the hand is allowed back in the stroke. It truly is remarkable to watch, and I would highly encourage you to attempt a similar progression and to watch the results this type of drilling with anti-paddles on the Tower produces.

Another example involving tennis balls and sprinting:

Six Rounds:

2 X 25 Swim with a Tech/EVF focus on the Power Tower, bucket filled 1/3 or less, whole stroke, with anti-paddles and snorkel

2 X 12.5 Max Blast Swim on the Power Tower, same weight, with snorkel and tennis balls

HANDS OUT

1 X 15 Max Blast Swim, no gear, no Power Tower

In a variation, we might have the first two 25s be left/right swim, or we might go left/right pull with much less water in the bucket. It would be impressive to see someone pull left/right with anti-paddles and the bucket filled with any substantial amount of water! This progression, again, is fantastic for teaching the brain to pull water with the forearm, and the final 15 Max Blast at full speed is quite impressive when the hand is allowed to anchor on "hard" water. I have found that athletes who normally cannot handle a deeper catch can and do in fact pull deeper and straighter after moving through a progression such as this one, and it lets me know that we are on the right track when it comes to improving technique and power in the stroke. This is more of a 50-yard freestyle drill as obviously you do not want mile types pulling too deep on the water, but every now and then I believe it is good for the longer types to get up and sprint a 15 with this type of stroke technique.

Some of our fastest ever 15s timed from a push to the head have been during sets such as these, and again this tells me that something good is happening when the athletes come off the anti-paddle work against resistance into free, untethered swimming. We often stretch the 15 to a 25, and the effect is the same: *fast* swimming, with the athletes anchoring on deep water and pushing faster times than they would otherwise. You have to see this kind of work to believe it, and I encourage you give it a try.

Another drill we love on the Power Tower and in untethered swimming is one we call fly pause drill, in which we break down the butterfly stroke into just the pull, with a pause at the catch before we initiate the stroke:

- We always go with a snorkel and a buoy. The paddle type if any will depend on the goal of the set.

- The overarching goal is achieving the EVF and training a straight pull, north to south.

- The recovery is always underwater.

- We teach the athletes to actually pause . . . pause and do not be afraid to take a look at the hands. Lift the head up and see if we have a great starting position of fingertips down, EVF, hands at shoulder width or slightly wider, elbows higher than wrist, and wrist higher than fingertips.

- We would obviously normally never have athletes lift the head to look at the hands. During this drill we do not mind, and we will use the GoPro to compare where the athletes saw their hands and where the HD GoPro saw their hands . . . my, how the two sometimes differ!

- This is a fantastic drill for free and fly types, especially sprinters, as the pulling pattern is quite similar in the two strokes.

This drill can be used for technique work, or as a pulling set for Pure Power and Power Endurance type work. I will list one example of each on the following pages.

Fly Pause for Tech:

Three Rounds:

8 X 25 On the Power Tower, fly pause with snorkel, buoy, and choice of training paddles, Tower filled with a minimal amount of water

1 X 50 Fly or free at 85-93%

As with the previous drills, the athletes feel incredible coming off the bucket, and the final 50 is quite fast, with little "muscle" in the stroke. Variations of the drill include using anti-paddles, tennis balls, or going sans paddles and using an open hand.

Fly Pause for Power Endurance:

Two Rounds:

6 X 100 On the Power Tower, fly pause drill, with buoy, snorkel, and choice of training paddles (we encourage our women to go with their largest paddles if they so desire)

1 X 50 Fly or free, Max, no Tower, no gear

As this is a Power Endurance set, we will have them pull fast or pull max-out effort, on a fast send off, with a decent amount of weight in the bucket. At this point, our women are only limited by how strong they are and by how much power endurance they currently have. Also of note, as the goal is Power Endurance, the pause would not be as long as it normally would on a fly pause Tower drilling set or on an untethered fly pause drill set.

Fly Pause for Pure Power:

Six Rounds:

3 X 12.5 Max Blast fly pause on the Tower, with buoy and snorkel, with a heavy bucket, with choice of training paddle

1 X 15 or 25 Max Blast swim, fly or free, with choice of gear

Pure Power fly pause with a heavy bucket is a challenge, but when our women can go heavy it certainly is a joy to watch from a coaching perspective. The pull must be incredibly strong here or they will go backwards on the Tower when one considers that they have no legs and they are recovering underwater. When your athletes can master fly pause for Pure Power with a heavy bucket you are going to see some fast sprint fly and free efforts when you add in the legs, and as with the previous sets, some of our fastest 15 and 25-yard fly and free efforts have come after heavy fly pause work. This set is yet another good example of Post-Activation Potentiation, and again I will speak more in-depth on the topic in chapter seven.

When comparing this type of work to the weight room or dry land, I think of it as quite similar to a Vasa Trainer workout, with the added benefit that the stroking patterns in fly pause against resistance more closely mimic those seen in untethered fly and free swimming than compared to what the Vasa can provide.

In a real world results example, our school record holder in the 100/200 fly here at Liberty went quite a bit of fly pause drill for tech, Power Endurance, and Pure Power on the Power Tower, and saw incredible time drops in our program in just two years with this type of training. She came in a 2:08 200 flyer and in just two those years dropped to a 1:56.7 before leaving Liberty after her sophomore year to return home to Australia to train for the 2016 Aussie Olympic Trials. She also dropped from 54.7 to 51.7 in the 100 fly, scoring 10th at NCAAs in 2014, and I believe much of these drops were the result of the hundreds of fly efforts she went against resistance on the Power Tower, the efforts being a mixture of Power Endurance, Pure Power, and a plethora of fly pause drill against the Tower mixed in.

Up until this point I have covered mostly free, fly, and back drills on the Power Tower, and it is certainly time I give the breaststrokers their chance to shine. Tower drilling is fantastic for breaststroke, and along with Yanko drill, the two drills outlined on the following pages are great for breaststroke and IM types. We subscribe to the Dave Salo "component style" of breaststroke training here at Liberty, and thus the only time we swim full stroke breaststroke is during race pace, dive quality sets, or Pure Power work on the Towers. We do not train Power Endurance full stroke breaststroke on the Towers as often as free or back as technique can suffer, but we do however love drilling breast on the Towers. It is quite easy to turn a drill set into a Power Endurance set, and we mix in a bit of both for our breaststrokers here at LU. Our two favorite breaststroke drills on the Tower:

Two or Three Kick, One Pull

This classic breaststroke drill certainly has added benefits on the Tower. As with the various drills for free, fly, and backstroke, if one is not moving forward on the Tower, they are moving backwards or are stationary, and again, as with the other drills, the Towers teach the breaststrokers to minimize any dead points in their kick or pull, with the goals of increasing distance per stroke, distance per kick, and of maintaining pressure on the water through the three (or four) phases of the pull. This drill is also great for teaching a fast kick recovery, as again, during the recovery phase of the kick the Tower is pulling them backwards, forcing the brain to subconsciously increase the kick tempo to keep the athlete moving forward.

Three Rounds:

8 X 25 Two or three kick, one pull, on the Tower, with little to no water, and no fins. The only paddles, if any, would be the yellow Finis Agility Paddles or a similar breaststroke paddle (fingertip paddles are great here). The pull should be performed at or just below race-pace velocity, while the kick should focus on the recovery tempo, again working on finishing with the feet together and achieving maximum distance per kick.

1 X 50 Going 25 two or three kick one pull / 25 whole stroke breast, both 25s at 85-93% (they might go a full 50 breast here as well)

We instruct the athletes to again count their strokes, with the goal of taking fewer strokes throughout the year with the same amount of water in the bucket or to maintain their stroke count (or decrease it, for the elite types) with a higher amount of water as they progress toward our conference meet in February. Distance per stroke and kick are emphasized, and we also instruct them to focus deliberately on minimizing dead periods in their stroke where they feel the Tower pulling them backwards. The added resistance will force them to streamline on the shoot forward recovery of the hands, as instinctively the brain will want to streamline tighter when resistance is added. I believe the propulsive phase of the kick encourages breaststrokers to become lazy at times—the kick provides so much propulsion that they often do not need to achieve streamline or full extension of the elbows on the recovery to feel as though they are moving forward. Such is not the case when resistance is added, as they must streamline during the recovery.

This drill is also fantastic for teaching them a narrow kick and narrow recovery on the kick, as the recovery of the kick is certainly one area where the Tower may pull them backwards or cause them to become stationary in the water if the kick recovery is too wide or the tempo is too slow. Two or three kick, one pull on the Tower is also a great drill to work on finishing the kick, as the athletes increase propulsion if they finish the kick, and this added propulsion from finishing the kick is a boost to the speed of the recovery of the kick, something we are always looking to improve.

As for the breaststroke pull, the Tower by default will force the athlete's brain to find a pulling pattern that maximizes propulsion, and whether more of a puller or a sculler with their arms, they will be forced to do either more efficiently and with more strength and power against resistance on the Tower.

We tend to break with Salo here at Liberty with regards to the pull, as we believe that a straighter pull stroke instead of a scull stroke is faster, especially for short-course yards. This is highly individual, however, and while we will not completely rebuild an athlete's pulling style if she is a true sculler, we will want her to incorporate a bit more of an actual backwards pulling motion into her stroke. That is to say, we would prefer the outsweep and the insweep of the pull to be a bit shorter, with more emphasis and time spent in a backwards, true pulling motion during the insweep.

Whereas Salo would advocate for outsweep, insweep, and recovery, we lean more toward four phases of the pull: outsweep, straight pull, insweep, recovery, with the pulling phase of the stroke being similar to that of a butterfly stroke or a Vasa Trainer movement. I should note that this backwards, straight pull phase of the stroke is extremely short, and a difference would be hard to see for the naked eye when compared to a more traditional triphasic stroke. Perhaps, then, we would say we want them to think about pulling backwards during the insweep of the pull; whether or not they actually achieve any straight north-to-south pulling is not something we could accurately measure.

I am one of the few coaches who does advocate for this straight pull, and I realize this is an unpopular stance. I do believe the pull can incorporate more north-to-south movement from the hands and elbows without sacrificing stroke rate; certainly the increase in frontal form drag is a concern that a coach will have to weigh against the added propulsion the pull provides. Having said as much, back to the Towers: Two or three kick one pull drill will improve the pull, kick, and recovery of the stroke and kick, regardless of whether the breaststroker is a sculler or more of a pulling type, and again, this is one of our favorite breaststroke drills on resistance.

The final breaststroke drill that I will cover is not so much a drill as a component of training, and that is pulling breaststroke on the Power Tower. Again, having referenced Salo's component theory, we pull quite a bit with our breast/IM types, and to say that Dave Salo has inspired a generation of coaches to think differently about breaststroke training is quite the understatement indeed. We pull breast with resistance and without, and pulling against resistance is fantastic for building strength, power, and endurance in the stroke, and as mentioned with the two kick one pull drilling, will teach the athletes' brains to instinctively find optimal stroking patterns that increase propulsion in the pull and decrease drag on the recovery of the arms.

Our breast pulling here at Liberty, both with resistance and without, is done in two ways, again borrowed from Salo. The first is what we call chair position, performed with a buoy and sometimes with a snorkel, where the athletes will "sit" in the water and pull breast in an upright position. This position is fantastic for isolating the pull, as there is absolutely no propulsion provided by the lower body. The second position is what we call regular, with a buoy and most often with a snorkel, where the athletes assume a regular breaststroke position and pull in a more traditional manner. This position will provide a bit of dolphin propulsion from the legs, even with a buoy, and for this reason we alternate between the two positions quite often.

Breaststroke pulling on the Power Tower is similar to the fly pause drill in that one can train for technique, Pure Power, or Power Endurance by changing the variables of the set. Three examples:

Breast Pulling for Tech:

Three Rounds:

8 X 25 Pull breast on the Power Tower, chair position, no water in the bucket, round one with anti-paddles, two with no paddles, three with the yellow Finis Agility Paddles (we have found this to be a fantastic breaststroke paddle)

1 X 50 Breast swim, no buoy, going 25 two kick one pull, 25 breast, at 85-93%

This type of drilling is again fantastic for developing the forearm component of the stroke, and we teach our breast/IM types to think of the entire forearm as a hand or a paddle that can be used to "grab water" during the outsweep, pull, and insweep of the stroke. We are following the same progression here as with the freestyle drills, where we take away the hand, add it back in, then increase the size of said hand as we progress through the rounds.

As you can tell by now, this is a theme that we use often here at Liberty, as I am firm believer that the brain learns much through the gear play involved with regards to pulling and learning to feel water on the hand. I believe the brain instinctively wants to pull on hard water, and when you take away the hand it will want to "switch" to the forearm and the upper arm to do so. Add the hand back in, and you have "increased" the size of the hand, in theory. This is a phenomenon that again needs to be seen to be believed, and the 50 breast going two kick one pull looks rather beautiful, for lack of a better term, when the athletes come off the Tower and into untethered, free swimming.

Breast Pulling for Power Endurance:

Six Rounds:

3 X 100 On the Power Tower, chair position, with the yellow Finis Agility Paddles, bucket filled 1/3 or less, going 95% effort breast pull, EZ backstroke, 100% effort breast pull, EZ backstroke by P.T. 25

This is a challenging set, to say the least! Whether Bernie Sanders fans or not, your athletes will certainly be feeling the burn on this set, and, again, this is fantastic for training Power Endurance into the breaststroke pull. As with the two kick one pull drill, the athletes are forced to recover in a tight streamline—perhaps more so because there is no propulsion coming from the legs. They simply must streamline during the recovery phase of the stroke in an attempt to save as much speed from the pull as possible before the Tower slows their forward momentum, stops them completely, or pulls them backwards depending on the amount of water in the bucket.

Breast Pulling for Pure Power:

Six Rounds:

3 X 12.5 Max Blast pull breast, choice chair or regular pull, heavy bucket (relative, as always), with choice of no paddles or the yellow Finis Agility Paddles

1 X 15 Max Blast swim breast, no Tower, Natural with no gear

Strength. Power. Speed. This type of "drill" will separate the strong from those who are not. There are no secrets and no shortcuts here, the athletes just need to anchor a hand on the water and hold on as they move through the three or four phases of the pull. As with Pure Power swimming, we are training the neuromuscular system here, with the goals of increasing maximum strength, recruiting more motor units, and recruiting more muscle fibers. Breaking down the barrier to maximum effort that is the Golgi Tendon System is another goal of Pure Power work in general; I look forward to the day when we understand further the ways in which we can train around this internal limiter.

Not many believe me, but our school-record holder in the 100/200 breast, Emilie Kaufman, could pull breast in the chair position for 12.5s with the bucket filled to 3/4, and there were days when she made it look easy. She could also swim full stroke breaststroke on Pure Power sets with a full bucket and routinely pulled more water on the Tower than some of our sprint freestylers. She split a 26.66 in the 50 breast in our 200 medley in 2014, and while some will disagree, yes, I do believe this is a case of causation and not just of correlation; the heavy Tower work she did over her two years here at Liberty (Emilie transferred in after two years at a Big Ten school) absolutely helped her to go faster.

A side note on pulling breaststroke: if you are not having your breast-strokers pull quite a bit in your program, I would advise you to start doing so, whether against resistance or not. If the words of Dave Salo and the above examples of Emilie Kaufman are not enough, consider the remarkable year that Indiana's Lilly King put together for further evidence of the impact that pulling breaststroke can have. In my humble opinion, King and Ray Looze at IU just authored the single best season in American female breaststroke history, doing the following:

- NCAA & American Record in the 100 Breast with a 56.85
- NCAA & American Record in the 200 Breast with a 2:03.59
- Sweep of the 100/200 Breaststroke at Trials

Furthermore, King had drops of:

- 59.6 to 56.8 in the 100 SCY
- 2:09.2 to 2:03.5 in the 200 SCY
- 1:07.9 to 1:05.2 in the 100 LCM
- 2:29.8 to 2:24.0 in the 200 LCM
- For good measure, she also threw in a 1:57.2 SCY 200 IM at Big Tens, dropping from a previous best of 2:00.9.

And . . . let us not forget her epic heroics in Rio, winning Olympic gold in a new OR, all while talking the talk and walking the walk, beating

Efimova in the process. (I had to delay the book during the final editing/printing process to add this!) And all of that comes from a 19-year-old college freshman. Dropping three seconds in the 100-yard breast over the course of an entire four-year college career is a feat . . . dropping three seconds in one season, when you're already a 59.6 breaststroker, is the stuff of legend, and Ray attributed much of King's success to breaststroke pulling in his talk at this year's College Swimming Coaches Association of America annual conference. To say that pulling breaststroke is important is certainly an understatement, and I believe wholeheartedly that breast pulling against resistance is a fantastic way to build power and endurance in the stroke.

I stated in the first section of this chapter that we often use Power Tower drills as part of a main set, and I will list several examples on the following pages. Tower drilling is fantastic for setting up a stroke that elicits easy speed when swimming unresisted, and there are few better ways to warm up the body and to ready the neuromuscular system for fast and efficient efforts in a workout.

Tower Drilling as Part of a Race-Pace Set:

Four Rounds:

150 On the Power Tower, with no water in the bucket or little water, with a snorkel, with Finis Agility Paddles

Free, Back, and Fly types: 25 left arm, 25 EZ Backstroke, 25 Right Arm, 25 EZ Backstroke, 25 whole stroke build, 25 EZ Backstroke

Breast types: a progression of 25 Yanko Drill, 25 Pull Regular, 25 2 kick 1 pull by Power Tower 25s, with the 25 on the way back always EZ backstroke

Unhook the Tower, rest 30 seconds, then right into:

6 X 50 @ 1:30, MAX, working on the 2nd 50 goal pace of the 100

Our women love this type of training, and they feel amazing, again for lack of a better term, on the first few 50s Max until the pain of lactate-tolerance training kicks in on the second half of the 6 X 50s.

Jake Shellenberger

Tower Drilling as Part of a Dive Quality Set:

Eight Rounds:

150 On the Power Tower, with no water or little in the bucket, no fins, with snorkel, buoy, and Finis Agility Paddles

Free, Fly types: 25 scull, 25 fly pause drill, 25 whole-stroke swim by Power Tower resisted 25

Back types: 25 scull, 25 double-arm backstroke, 25 whole-stroke swim by Power Tower 25

Breaststroke types: 25 scull, 25 Yanko Drill, 25 three kick one pull

Unhook the Tower, walk to the start end of the pool (important here not to swim to the start end . . . we want the first swim effort off the Tower to be the dive max effort)

1 X 50 Dive MAX for time with touch pads in!

The touchpads will elicit faster swimming by default, but the Tower drilling certainly helps to set up the stroke as well! In another dive-quality example, this one focusing solely on the EVF and pulling water with the forearm:

12 Rounds:

200 On the Power Tower, with no water in the bucket, with snorkel and Finis anti-paddles, no fins, with free and fly types swimming freestyle, going the four Power Tower 25s descend 1-2, 3-4 to 75% effort

Back types would swim back the same way with no snorkel, and breast types would again descend the PT 25s 1-2 and 3-4, but would go 25 three kick one pull on the first 25 and two kick one pull on the second effort.

Unhook the Tower with Anti-Paddles STILL ON.

HANDS OUT! Exit the pool like an athlete.

Walk to the start end.

Dive 25 Max, free and back types to a foot touch

The previous two dive-quality sets elicit *fast* swimming, and it is fun to watch from the deck as the athletes grab a large amount of water on that 25 Dive Max. After a 200 against resistance on the Power Tower with anti-paddles, the brain is hungry to pull on some hard water, and again our women feel as though their hands are huge and as though they are pulling on concrete when the hands are allowed back into the stroke. While the aforementioned sets are largely for sprint types, the mid-distance and distance types can benefit from this type of Power Tower drilling into a dive-quality set; perhaps a 200/500 type would go a broken 200 following the Power Tower efforts instead of a dive 50 or dive 25.

I mentioned in the opening of this chapter I would list several drills that I believe are detrimental to sprint freestyle, drills that sprinters, in my humble opinion, should stop practicing immediately. This was not always the plan, as the intent during my original brainstorming sessions for this section was to focus solely on the positive aspects of drilling with resistance. Having said as much, I do believe we are doing our sprinters at the club and college level a disservice by continuing to teach the following drills. On a selfish note, I also have to spend a good deal of time and energy correcting the stroke errors these drills can cause. Thus, for the sake of our sprint athletes and for the time of every college sprint coach, I will list what I believe are the top five worst drills for sprint freestyle and why sprinters at every level should discontinue their practice.

1. Fingertip Drag

Perhaps we rename this drill the anti-straight-arm-recovery drill. I would rather teach sprinters a high elbow catch than a high elbow recovery, and I believe this drill actually reinforces a low elbow on said catch. Fingertip drag also teaches the athletes to enter the hand into the water well before the ideal distance per stroke is achieved, and as such, forces them to slide the hand forward after the entry in order to achieve distance on the stroke. This, of course, increases drag tremendously, and we never want our sprinters here at Liberty moving their hands forward in the water for a 50 free.

Fingertip drag as demonstrated by our assistant coach, Jessica Barnes.

We see Jessica's entry in the next image.

I would rather we not reinforce this entry for our sprint free types. We see the elbow actually hitting the water before the fingertips—a cause of drag in the recovery of the stroke.

We also want an early vertical forearm with the high elbow, and I believe it is harder to develop a fingertips-down entry and EVF when "attacking" the entry from an already low point in the recovery, as fingertip drag teaches. I never saw the point in this drill for sprinters, and no coach has been able to convince me this drill benefits sprint types to the point where we should include this drill over others. If we say *yes* to a drill, we say *no* to another, and there are much better alternatives for teaching hip rotation for a hip-driven stroke, if that is the goal.

2. Catch-Up Free

I believe this is the single worst drill for sprinters, and I am sure I will catch a bit of ire, as this is also one of the most popular of all freestyle drills. Similar to fingertip drag, I believe this drill teaches everything we would rather not want to see in sprint free:

1. Teaches elbow lower than wrist on the catch
2. Teaches wrist lower than fingertips on the catch
3. Teaches the athlete to slide the hand forward to the catch through the water

I do not want to see sprint types "laying out" on their side with their hand above the elbow. This survival stroke is great for making it through 20 X 200s, but perhaps not so great for beating Florent Manaudou in a 50 free.

Jessica halfway through the recovery phase of catch-up drill

I should note that Jessica was not exaggerating this position for the book, as this is the natural position a swimmer takes when rotated on the side and moving through catch-up drill. Proponents of catch-up will debate that it teaches distance per stroke, but the sheer physics of such an argument holds no water when one stops to think about what is actually happening when we use this drill. As a simple case in point, would fly be fast if we recovered underwater? Would freestyle be fast if we recovered underwater? Why then, would we teach a freestyle where some of the recovery is underwater? And by recovery underwater, let us define recovery as any part on the stroke that is moving in the same direction as the athlete . . . any force that is not a drag or lift-propulsion force.

As for distance per stroke, I would rather teach DPS above the water, through air resistance, than through the water, a medium 784 times denser than air. When prescribing catch-up drill, we are essentially asking our athletes to substitute a much faster out-of-water recovery for a slower underwater recovery.

The catch-up drill entry. Notice the position of the right arm—why would we want to reinforce this position?

3. N-Kick Switch With Arm Fully Extended

The key reason I do not like this drill for sprint types is the position of the arm fully extended while the swimmer is on the side. This, once again, teaches a low elbow catch, with the elbow in a position below the wrist and below the fingertips. A coach may instruct the athlete to maintain the fingertips below the elbow, however if the athlete is fully extended on her side I believe these attempts are futile, as this position is extremely hard to hold for any extended period of time. I do think this drill has benefits when performed with the extended arm in the early vertical forearm/catch position, not fully extended, with the elbow clearly above the wrist. We do prescribe such a drill here at LU, calling it "N-Kick Catch Switch," and we are careful to pay special attention to details here, as we want to maintain the correct EVF and high-elbow position.

4. Fist Drill

This may come as a shock, as I love anti-paddle work, but as with tennis balls the athletes tend to cheat here or to lose focus, and the result is a waste of time for both coach and athlete. Even if the athletes maintain extreme focus and swim this drill with a tight fist, one can still get a decent amount of propulsion from the flat surface the fist creates, again defeating the purpose of the drill. I do not believe we train the brain nearly as well with the fist as we do the anti-paddle. Thus, let us use the anti-paddle whenever possible.

We also want the athletes focusing on a high elbow and an early vertical forearm with a relaxed hand, not using valuable cognitive resources focusing on keeping the fist tight. (I want the brain to forget about the hand altogether . . . put it to sleep!) The idea of opportunity cost is crucial here; if a coach says *yes* to fist drill they say *no* to anti-paddles. Time is limited, and so are drill sets for the majority of coaches. We like to make every drill and every stroke count here at LU—think of the effect over four years in a college program! While, yes, exaggerated for the book, you will see the position below often when prescribing fist drill:

5. Fingertips to Shoulder Touch on the Recovery

See fingertip drag, as these are similar drills.

In closing, I believe the Power Towers are fantastic for drilling and tech swimming, and I believe there are immense benefits to be realized for every distance and every stroke. Technical flaws, other inefficiencies in the kick or elsewhere, and balance issues in the stroke can be more easily identified against resistance, and with the addition of said resistance the brain is forced to figure out how to move through the water faster and more efficiently. Anti-paddles, in my humble opinion, are the best tech paddles our sport has to offer, and their benefits are, again, magnified against resistance on the Tower. I encourage you to experiment here, as the drills and sets I have shared above are just the beginning of what we do here at Liberty, and the possibilities are endless for the creative types who find enjoyment in drill creation and so forth.

Chapter 6: Kicking

"If you have a leg problem, well, you have an arm problem."

Nolan Ryan

I DEBATED whether to include kicking in the previous chapters on Pure Power and Power Endurance or to cover kicking as a whole in a separate chapter. Ultimately, I decided that because underwater body dolphin is of the utmost importance, yes, an entire chapter dedicated to resistance training with the legs would be in order. My guess is that the majority of coaches reading this work will utilize the ideas contained herein more often for the short-course season, and as we know, the fifth stroke, underwater body dolphin, is ultimately what separates the elite from the great and the great from the good in the short pool.

For events 200 and under, you will be hard-pressed to find elite athletes in the short-course yard format who are not also elite underwater, and a trip to the NCAA championship meet any given year reveals the power of the fifth stroke in full force.

Simply put, if your athletes swim the 200 or under, of any stroke, and you want them to achieve elite-level status in our sport, they simply must be great underwater, not just good, with breaststroke occasionally being the exception (although even that is changing, as the best breaststrokers are quite elite with their underwater work in their own right). While not everyone can or will achieve the elite level, if the goal for your athletes is simply to come as close as is humanly possible to reaching their full genetic potential, maximizing the speed at which they travel underwater must play a role. I submit to you that even if they swim faster than they currently kick underwater due to body dolphin technique or to hip/knee/ankle flexibility issues, these flaws should be corrected if possible—I would not advise giving up on dolphin kicking, from the age-group swimmer all the way to the college level (severe physical limitations are the exception).

The Power Tower, as you may have guessed, is a fantastic tool for training the dolphin kick, and both speed and endurance can be developed using Pure Power and Power Endurance training techniques. We train a great amount of underwater work on the Power Towers here at Liberty, and we focus on underwater body dolphin quite a bit in general, both on the Towers and off.

Disclaimer:

At the time of this writing, our sport has been plagued by recent unfortunate events involving breath-holding competitions and shallow-water blackouts. The sets, ideas, and philosophies outlined in this chapter are geared toward our elite-level college women, and even then, we are extremely careful with the underwater work we prescribe. The intelligent coach would certainly tailor the sets and ideas listed here, as needed, when working with a different audience. Again, these sets are geared toward elite college athletes. Coach and train at your own risk.

- No, we do not attempt underwater 100s and so forth here at LU.
- No, we are not interested in how far our women can travel underwater.
- We are not training for free diving or training to set breath-holding records.
- We do not test for breath holding nor do we test for distance traveled underwater.
- Be smart, use common sense, and train at your own risk when prescribing underwater work!

Having said as much, we do however train to hold our underwater body dolphins off the last wall in a 100 and the last few walls in a 200, and the reality of our sport in the short-course yard format is that the fastest athletes are pushing the limits of underwater swimming, and doing so does in fact require training the body in workouts to handle a higher CO_2 level in the blood. This is an objective fact in our sport that we *must* balance with the risks that underwater swimming entails. The lifeguards and safety folks reading this are no doubt up in arms by now, but, again, the fastest way to move through water is the underwater body dolphin. We are allowed to do so for 15 meters off each wall, and we must train safely to do so if we want to swim as fast as is possible for humans to swim.

What, then, is a coach to do? How can we train the body to travel as close to 15 meters off each wall as is possible, while doing so in a safe manner? Common sense, logic, and a keen eye in workouts are key. A coach needs to know his or her athletes, their underwater abilities, and their current levels of CO_2 buffering capacity, and the coach must also have a clear understanding of how challenging any given set would be for each specific athlete.

I am amazed, at times, when I hear some of the sets out there that have been prescribed to "train" underwater kicking. Not only are many of them nearly impossible for all but a few of the most elite athletes, a coach must be extremely cautious when prescribing such a set to "type A" personalities who will push the limits to make them. This is when accidents happen, and while pushing limits is a good thing, in general, a coach simply *must* know and respect the individual physiological differences among athletes when prescribing underwater sets. As a simple example, we do not expect our freshmen in September or October to handle the underwater sets that our returning athletes can make, and we are not afraid to prescribe different sets for said freshmen or to modify existing sets in our early-season training.

With my disclaimer out of the way, let me say again that underwater and body dolphin training in general is important in our sport. We can improve underwater kicking on Power Tower so let us get back to it. There are numerous examples in our sport of underwater greatness, and I will share just a few below to drive home the importance of this often overlooked piece of the swim training puzzle.

I had the privilege (and what a privilege it was) to be on deck coaching our Penn State sprinters at the men's NCAA championship meet in 2009, at the height of, and the last NCAA championship meet of, the infamous suit era, and, again, what a privilege indeed. While there were a plethora of incredible swims, the one I thought was the most impressive was Austin Staab's 44.18 American record and now-former NCAA record in the 100-yard fly. Not only did he kick to 15 off the last wall, he swam the entire last 25 no breath to the finish. There are some who said he swam the entire race no breath, breathing only at the walls, and while I have not confirmed this, I would believe it possible. Again, this requires incredible training to accomplish, and while the safety folks might say Staab was crazy for attempting such a feat, they must call him a former NCAA and current American record holder before they call him crazy. The cerebral coach will certainly recognize that Austin and his coaches no doubt spent countless hours of training, four years' worth, building up to that swim, and I am sure they were highly calculated in their workouts along the way.

Patrick Schirk, the aforementioned NCAA champion in the 200 backstroke, kicked 12.5 yards underwater off each wall in his winning effort, and many NCAA champions before and since in the 200 fly and 200 back have been 12.5 or more off each of their walls. David Nolan's American and NCAA record of 1:39.38 in the 200 IM at NCAAs in 2015 was swum halfway underwater, as was Jack Conger's 1:39.31 200-fly time trial, the American and then NCAA record from the Big 12 championship meet of the same year. Legendary Texas coach Eddie Reese said of Conger's fly, "I told him he was going to get tired . . . just stay underwater and keep kicking" (SwimSwam 2015).

Conger has since gone faster, 1:38.06 at this year's 2016 NCAA championships, and again the swim was an example of underwater mastery of the highest level.

And as for the 200 backstroke, our American and NCAA record of 1:35.73, also set at the men's NCAAs in 2016 by Ryan Murphy of Cal, was also swum halfway underwater, with Murphy blowing away the field and kicking out to 12.5 off each wall en route to his record win. Let us not forget Murphy's inconceivable 43.49 100-back from this year as well, again showing his incredible speed underwater. And the list goes on. Natalie Coughlin's 100-back NCAA and American record of 49.97, Liz Pelton's NCAA-record and American-record 200 back of 1:47.84, Kelsi Worrell's 100-fly NCAA and American record of a staggering 49.43, and so on and so forth . . . all had in common elite-level underwaters, not just in distance off the wall—they were also kicking *fast*.

A simple commandment: You must be elite underwater if you want to be an elite short-course-yards swimmer. While there may be a few exceptions here and there, we should be careful not to use a few exceptions to try to prove the rule. The magic happens underwater, and you must train to be elite underwater if you want to be elite in the strokes in the short pool.

As such, we train underwater body dolphin quite a bit on the Towers and with other resistance toys, training for speed with Pure Power sets and for speed endurance and for the ability to hold our underwaters longer with Power Endurance work. By quite a bit, I insist that we do, in fact, dedicate a lot of time to training underwater and do not simply pay lip service to said training.

I remember a phone conversation with a recruit during which she mentioned that her club team focused a lot on underwater work. I asked how much, and she said they did a few 25s underwater at the end of practice two or three times a week. I chuckled a bit and, as she was a backstroker, asked her if she knew the fastest way to move through water. She replied, "Dolphin kicking."

"Well done" I said. I then followed up with a second question: "And how much of your 100 back are you allowed to kick underwater?"

She replied, "Fifteen meters off each wall." So far, so good.

I then asked a question relating to school: "If your teacher gave you a study guide for a test, and sixty percent of the test material covered a certain subject matter that is 'hard' or challenging information with which you are unfamiliar, and the other forty percent covered different, but well-known material, where you would spend the majority of time studying?"

A rhetorical question, she obviously answered that she would spend the most time on the sixty percent of the material with which she was unfamiliar. I then explained to her my point:

> Yes, underwater body dolphin is the fastest way to move through the water, and you are allowed to swim 60 meters underwater in your 100 backstroke. This converts to roughly 65 yards, a whopping 65% of the race. Going back to the school test material metaphor, certainly if you had an upcoming test and 65% of the subject matter was on an unfamiliar topic, while 35% was on a different but well-known topic, you would spend a lot of time making sure that you knew the 65% of unfamiliar material by heart. [talking to a 17-year-old girl] Tell me, then, do your coaches

spend 65% of your 100-back training focusing on underwater body dolphin, an area that is uncomfortable and "hard" for most athletes?

There was silence on the other end as she contemplated the logic and reason contained in the concept I laid out before her. She got it, and every time I use this analogy with a fly or back recruit, specifically, they instinctively "get it." Their coaches are spending a lot of time training them in fly and back, yes, but not a lot of time on their underwaters, the fastest way to move through the water and an area where we can spend 65% of our race (and should if we want to be elite, as proven).

When I say then that we spend a lot of time training underwater body dolphin here at Liberty, I mean it wholeheartedly. It amazes me the amount of coaches who simply do not do this, when the overwhelming evidence is that it *is* that important, but that is another book for another time.

We have had athletes here at Liberty, mainly sprint-freestyle types whose third event was a 100 fly or a 100 back, drop significant amounts of time in said fly and back races without training stroke. They simply improved their underwaters and became more comfortable with the pain and discomfort that comes with maxing out the underwater portion of the race. One such example is Brye Ravettine, our school-record holder in the 50 free. Her training focus here was mainly sprint freestyle, but she saw great drops in her 100 back over her career by working underwater body dolphin on Pure Power and Power Endurance sets on the Power Tower. Brye entered our program with high-school times of 23.2 and 51.7 in the freestyles and 57.2 in the 100 back, she and graduated with times of 22.1, 49.2, and 54.5 in the back, spending little time training "traditional" backstroke throughout her career.

She did, however, train backstroke quite often if using a different reference point, as I estimate she went roughly 250-300 X 12.5 Max Blast underwater body dolphin kick efforts with a heavy bucket on the Power Tower per year, with over a thousand such efforts in her career. Having said as much, certainly using resistance and Power Towers specifically is not the only way to train underwaters, but I do believe it is one of the best.

The opposite can also be true; stroke types can improve sprint freestyle mainly by improving their frontside underwaters on the Power Tower without training much sprint freestyle. An example would be our previously mentioned school-record holder in the 100/200 fly, Jessica Reinhardt, who entered our program with times of 54.7 in the 100 fly, 2:08 in the 200 fly, and 24.2/52.4 in the 50/100 free. As she was mainly a flyer, she did not train much sprint freestyle specifically, but she went the same estimated 250-300 X 12.5s Max Blast underwater body dolphin kick efforts on the Power Tower with a heavy bucket each year over the course of her two years here at Liberty. She left with times of 22.7 in the 50 and 50.1 in the 100 free, and she was certainly unique in that she played significant roles in our four sprint relays as a 100/200-fly type . . . rare!

Our Power Tower kicking is performed with both a Pure Power and a Power Endurance focus, with 200-stroke and 200/400-IM types focusing more on Power Endurance and with 100-stroke and sprint-free types focusing more on Pure Power. The sets and reps for Pure Power work are similar to Pure Power swimming, while Power Endurance kicking is performed quite differently than Power Endurance swimming. A few sample sets:

Pure Power Kicking:

Note: The bucket weight will depend on whether or not we are wearing fins, as athletes can obviously handle more water when wearing fins. We go a mixture of Tower kicking with and without regular and mono fins, for several reasons:

1. By not wearing fins we keep the athlete's feet connected to the water, and as with the hands, we attempt to teach the athletes to feel water on the feet when they swim. Good swimmers "feel" and hold on to water with their hands . . . great athletes do so with their hands *and* feet. We want them to consciously think about such things when they kick, and Pure Power efforts sans fins are a great place for the athletes to focus on grabbing water with the feet while kicking against resistance.

2. With fins and especially with the monofin, we can elicit a greater neuromuscular response from the brain/body, as we have increased the surface area and size of the feet, recruiting more motor units and muscle fibers in the legs and core in the process. Pure Power efforts with fins and a heavy bucket also elicit a major Post-Activation Potentiation response, and as with Pure Power swimming, some of our fastest timed kick efforts have been post heavy bucket kicking with fins. In my humble opinion, without

having conducted any controlled studies with our women, the fins and heavier bucket are needed to elicit a true Post-Activation Potentiation response; we simply do not see the same "pop" in the kick without wearing fins.

Six Rounds:

3 X 12.5 Max Blast underwater body dolphin kick on the Power Tower, with a heavy bucket and fins

1 X 15 Max Blast underwater body dolphin kick, no Tower, no fins, for time

In a variation of this set, we would keep fins on for the 15 max kick and would see some great leg/hip action from the women after the heavy bucket efforts. Post-Activation Potentiation is real, and while, again, I have not performed any legitimate experiments, the watch seldom lies; our fastest 15-meter kick efforts with and without fins have nearly always come after heavy bucket kick efforts. It is a joy to watch!

As with Pure Power swimming, this kind of training can also be included with a main set for a Race Pace or Dive Quality workout, with two examples below:

Pure Power Kicking With Dive Quality:

12 Rounds:

3 X 12.5 Max Blast underwater body dolphin kick on the Power Tower, Heavy bucket (relative, as always to the individual), with fins

Unhook the Tower, fins off, walk to the start end

1 X 25 Dive Max, no fins, with race specific number of underwater dolphins on the start, free and back types to a foot touch, odd rounds from a flat start, even rounds from a relay start

Each woman knows her ideal number of dolphin kicks off the start, and by timing breakouts, the head to 15 meters, and the final 25, we can see the power of the Towers at work. The three aforementioned times are nearly always faster after the Tower efforts than if we had done the set without.

In a variation, we might throw on a heavy weight belt in addition to the Power Tower on the odd rounds; this adds another level of resistance the athletes must overcome and once again elicits a *fast* dive effort on the 25 max. In still another variation we might go 2 X 25s dive max, the first with a weight belt and the second without.

Pure Power Kicking with Race Pace:

Four Rounds:

2 X 12.5 Max Blast underwater body dolphin kick on the Power Tower, heavy bucket, no fins

Rest 30 Seconds, unhook the Tower, refocus and regroup

12 X 25 @:30 Max Blast swim, working race specific number of dolphins, pushing off the wall like an athlete

Note: Pushing off the wall like an athlete—I borrowed this one from former Franklin and Marshall Head Coach Bob Rueppel. I got to know him during my college days at Shippensburg while I was an assistant in the summers at Trident Swim Club (now Diplomat Swim Club), my own club team based in my hometown of Lancaster, Pennsylvania. Bob, now the head coach at Middlebury College in Middlebury, Vermont, would always have his swimmers "push off the wall like an athlete" for any race-pace or fast efforts, and we do the same here at Liberty.

The concept: In all four strokes we never push off the wall in the front position off the turn; we are always on the side or in a quarter-twist position. Leaving the wall like an athlete, then, mimics the turn—each athlete leaving on her side, rotated forty-five to ninety degrees, with one hand on the wall, practicing coming off the wall in a quarter or half turn, as in a race. As we know, dolphin kicking underwater is faster on the side; thus, not only are we practicing a half or quarter turn in the process, we are in fact pushing of the wall faster than we would if we simply dropped down underwater on the front, as seen on the next page.

The true athletes also get a bit of stretch-reflex theory involved in the push off, as they will "load up" on the wall before pushing off, similar to the downward movement during a vertical jump test before pushing off the ground. If your athletes are having trouble mastering this technique, simply have them demonstrate vertical jump mechanics on the deck and ask them transfer to the water.

In the following sequence, we see our assistant coach Jessica Barnes pushing off the wall in an athletic manner. For whatever reason, our women tend to loathe having to push of the wall this way for fast efforts, but it allows them to work race-specific numbers of dolphins off the wall, on their sides, from a turn position. As an example, if a sprint freestyler takes five dolphin kicks off the turn in a race, in the example set previously listed, she would take the first three kicks off the wall of each 25 effort on her side, using the final two body dolphins to transition to the front side as she begins her freestyle flutter kicks into the breakout.

Jake Shellenberger

Our athletes have everything to gain and nothing to lose by pushing off the wall this way, and while, yes, it is "annoying" at times to have to remember to push off the wall as though an athlete, it trains them to be faster swimmers and works race-specific skills and details. As Bill Dorenkott used to say at Penn State, "We aren't here for your entertainment, we are here to make you better student-athletes!"

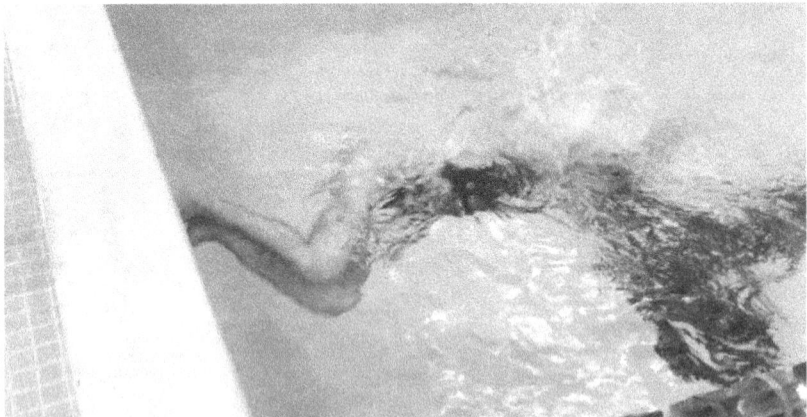

Power Endurance Kicking:

Our 200 of stroke, IM, and 400-IM types focus more on Power Endurance kicking on the Towers and with resistance; however this type of work is great for 100-fly and back types to train coming off the last two walls as well. We want our women to own these last two walls in a race, and it is a mentality that few possess instinctively—for the majority of athletes, I believe it must be taught. Power Endurance kicking is performed with and without fins, with generally more performed without fins, as the bucket is not nearly as heavy as it is with a Pure Power focus. A few sample sets, with some main set ideas mixed in:

Three Rounds:

8 X 12.5 Max Blast underwater body dolphin, on the Power Tower with bucket filled 1/3 or less, with no fins, on a 25-second send-off (The athletes must get back to the wall quickly to make the send-off, and the short rest interval ensures we are training for the endurance aspect of the kick.)

Unhook the Tower, right into:

1 X 50 Push Max, working race-specific number of dolphin kicks off the walls

This can be an extremely tough set depending on the amount of water in the bucket, the efficiency of the pulleys, and the skill level and CO_2 buffering capacity of the athletes performing the set. By the fifth 12.5 effort they are approaching a heart rate and CO_2 level in the blood that mimics almost perfectly the last wall of a 100 and the last three walls of a 200. Efforts five through eight are where the real training adaptations take place, and while certainly uncomfortable and quite painful, I believe it is important that stroke types go to this place often, even better if on the Towers against resistance. As we saw from the real-world American and NCAA record examples previously mentioned, the ability to kick (and kick fast), off the last wall in a 100 and the last three walls in a 200 can make or break the race, and, again, we want our women attacking this kind of set with the mentality that they own the last wall.

The 50 Max to finish the round then allows them to "put the Tower efforts into something that looks like fast swimming," to quote Rick DeMont, and while that 50 effort is rarely close to a best-time push effort, there is a massive training effect taking place as they hold their underwaters off the two walls in the 50. This gives them the confidence to do so in a race, and, again, this is a mentality that I believe can and should be trained; as much as we wish it were so, we as coaches should not expect our athletes to have this "X-factor" by default.

Speaking of mentality, many of us have heard of the many great distance sets noted in the chapter on Power Endurance that play a role in changing distance athletes' confidence levels and psyche, and the legendary sets of Erik Vendt and the "Animal Lane" of Mark Schubert's Mission Viejo squads of the 1970s are two that come to mind. Brian Goodell has spoken at length about how these now epic Schubert workouts helped shape his unbending will and distance acumen, and while the 12.5s on the Tower certainly pale in comparison to 10 X 1500 and so forth, they are challenging in their own right, and I believe they play a large role in developing the confidence to "stay underwater and keep kicking" as Eddie Reese told Jack Conger before his then-American/NCAA-record 200 fly from 2015. Owning the last few walls is a mindset, one formed by hours upon hours of challenging workouts and training the body to handle extreme CO2 levels in the blood, and, again, I believe the Tower is a fantastic way to develop this underwater resiliency.

As always, Power Endurance kicking sets can be included within main sets for an even greater effect, and I will list two examples for mid-distance and distance types:

Power Endurance Kicking With Broken Dive Quality For 200/500 Freestyle Types:

Two Rounds:
12 X 12.5 Max Blast underwater body dolphin, no fins, with the bucket filled 1/3 or less on a 25-second send off

Unhook Tower, 25 EZ to the start end @ 40 seconds

Dive 100 at 500 take out @ 1:20 to a foot touch

Push 3 X 100 @ 1:20 to a foot touch, MAX

Push 50 MAX @ :40 to a foot touch

Push 50 MAX - Bring it Home!

We must certainly not overlook the importance of underwater body dolphin for 500 types in a short course pool, and although the type of Power Endurance kicking described here is more geared toward 200-stroke types, distance freestylers can also benefit. In a Liberty-specific example, our best 500 athlete this past year was also a great 200 flyer in her club days, and she takes three to four dolphin kicks off each wall in her 500. With nineteen turns, let us estimate she is taking some sixty underwater body dolphin kicks during her 500, and there is much time to drop by making sure those sixty kicks are as fast as possible while also staying efficient from a physiological cost standpoint. We want our distance types to kick off their walls, but not to "waste" the legs while doing so. Training the body dolphin while under stress in a set such as this one will go a long way toward achieving this goal, and even more so if the athletes work those three to four dolphin kicks on the swim efforts when they remove the Tower.

This 500 athlete was also our best miler, and the cumulative effects of these dolphin kicks are obviously magnified over the longer distance. This example again proves that the Power Tower is much more than a toy for sprint freestyle and stroke types, as distance swimmers can also benefit from specific Power Endurance kicking on the Towers. The dolphin kick is a weapon of sorts, and the distance swimmer who can master said kick will have an advantage coming off the last few falls in the 500 and mile races.

Power Endurance Kicking As Part of Race-Pace Training for 200 Fly/Back/IM Types:

Three Rounds:

12 X 12.5 Max Blast underwater body dolphin, no fins, with the bucket filled 1/3 or less @ :25

Unhook Tower, 20 seconds rest to regroup and refocus

8 X 50 @ :50 Max or holding 200 Pace, with race-specific number of dolphin kicks off each wall

This type of set is fantastic for 200-stroke and IM types, with the strokers going all 8 X 50s the same stroke, while the IM types might perform the set with rolling IM 50s or go all 8 X 50 as 25 breast/25 free, working on hammering the underwater dolphin kicks off the breast turn and into the freestyle on the way home. We do quite a bit of this work here at Liberty, and for as much as we talk about sprinting and are known as a sprint program, at the time of this writing we own our conference's record in the 200 fly, not in the 50 or 100 free.

As always, the possibilities with Pure Power and Power Endurance kicking sets are endless, and we as coaches are only limited by our creativity and our athletes' willingness to work when we are dreaming up Tower kicking sets. Again, the Power Tower is much more than a tool for 50 freestyle types, and I trust the aforementioned sets will go a long way in opening up the coaching community to the potential of the Towers. I do believe we have much left to explore!

Chapter 7: Post-Activation Potentiation

"You take a piece of metal and you bend it and you let it go. He has a lot of that in his start. He's got a lot of deadlift, meaningful deadlift in his start."

Rick DeMont on Roland Schoeman's start

I HAVE mentioned Post-Activation Potentiation (henceforth PAP) several times thus far in the preceding six chapters, and I am thrilled to now pen the following section on PAP in-depth. I believe wholeheartedly that, not only does PAP deserve its own chapter, one could write an entire book on PAP alone and the potential that lies therein, if they so desired. PAP is simple in theory, yet ultimately complex when one attempts to break down the why, how, what, and when to include PAP in a training program.

Swimming coaches have been implementing PAP in their body of work instinctively for many years without knowing it; if you have ever prescribed a pre-race warm up with resisted or assisted stretch cord efforts, you have experimented with a form of Post-Activation Potentiation. The beauty, mystery, and excitement of PAP is that simple cord pulls are just the tip of the iceberg, so to speak, as this form of training is limitless in its application to swimming and especially to sprint training. While PAP can and should be used for mid-distance and distance types in practice and in meets to elicit the desired neuromuscular responses and in turn an increase in speed, the payoff is certainly greater for sprint types of all strokes.

What is PAP, then, and how does it work? Simply put, PAP is a movement or exercise combined with a stimulus meant to produce a specific neuromuscular response, followed by a similar movement or exercise without the stimulus, with the goal of a "better" performance post-stimulus. In the most basic example from the strength-training world, we might see resisted squats combined with a vertical jump or weighted box jumps with a weight vest followed by a box jump without a vest. In swimming we see countless examples, many of which I will outline in this chapter, including

Power Tower efforts into efforts with no Tower and the aforementioned stretch cord assisted and resisted efforts seen during meet preparation and in training.

The strength training, the track and field, and the little research we have in the swimming community is nearly universal in its agreement that PAP training does elicit better (faster, higher, stronger, farther, etc.) efforts post stimulus, and the implications are many, not only for meet performance and pre-race preparation, but for training as well. For what it is worth, we in the swimming community lag behind the track and strength-training science in regards to PAP research, and I would love to see more coaches and sport scientists approach the topic; I do believe there is much we can learn by exploring the limits of PAP training through official research channels and good old fashioned coach-athlete experimentation.

For an introduction into the science behind PAP from a swimming-specific study, I would encourage the reader to consult Andrew Hancock's "Effect of Post-Activation Potentiation on Swim Sprint Performance," which Andrew submitted as part of his Master's of Education in Exercise Science from Cleveland State in 2012. Andrew swam for Cleveland State and has since moved into the coaching ranks; similar to me, he started the swimming & diving program at West Florida from scratch in 2012 after coaching at his alma mater for five years.

It is deep into the training where I will focus the majority of my efforts in this chapter, as cord work for meets is a widely accepted practice and rather elementary in the PAP world. That is to say, I am not sure what more value I could bring to the meet preparation discussion that we do not already know; a sprint assisted or resisted effort pre-race will cause a PAP effect, and the athlete will (more often than not) swim faster than if the PAP effort had not been performed. Again, we have known this for years in the coaching community and have been prescribing PAP instinctively for quite some time. Having said as much, I will offer some pre-race tips and tricks that we implement here at Liberty, the goal being to give you something new with which to experiment in your program.

Getting back to the training, the training presents a brave new world, and later in this chapter I will outline some thoughts and theories that will test the limits of athletes, coaches, and even facilities in our never ending quest for ever faster performances. I believe in earnest that it is deep within the training where PAP will have the greatest impact in our sport as we unravel its many mysteries in the years to come.

First, a few thoughts on meet preparation:

"If I had any courage, I would ship Power Towers to the Big Ten meet."

Bill Dorenkott, circa 2008, Then Head Swimming & Diving Coach at Penn State University

Yes, Post-Activation Potentiation elicits responses so great in swimming that Bill half-joked about shipping Power Towers to the Big Ten championship meet so that our student-athletes could warm up with them as desired without the need for a coach or a cord. Bill and I saw some amazing performances after PAP work in practices at PSU and instantly became believers in the awesome power of this tool for both acute pre-race meet preparation and for long-term adaptation in training. As PAP for meet preparation is the most popular form and the most widely utilized, I will start the discussion here.

Again, we in the coaching community have been using PAP for many years instinctively, both in the form of assisted and resisted cord efforts in workouts and as part of a pre-race routine. At major meets, such as Olympic Trials, you will even find a dedicated stretch cord lane, and I applaud USA Swimming's decision to have such a lane, as assisted cord work can certainly be dangerous in a crowded warm-up pool with athletes moving at faster-than-competition speeds.

Track coaches were some of the first to experiment with assisted efforts in the form of towing and downhill running, and we in the swimming community owe our initial PAP experimentation with stretch cords to the work of the track community. The theory is simple, yet the underlying science is a bit more complex, as I previously stated. The resisted and assisted cord efforts "light up" the neuromuscular system, for lack of a better term, with the effects and subsequent increased performance window lasting anywhere from right after to fifteen minutes after the initial stimulus, depending on which study you choose to believe. Here at Liberty, we aim for ten to twelve minutes prior to the start of the race, for

Jake Shellenberger

several reasons. I will highlight what I believe are the most important three:

1. Of the many studies I have read detailing PAP throughout the track, strength-training, and swimming literature, nearly all have indicated that the neuromuscular system is still primed ten minutes after the initial PAP effort(s). That is to say, nearly all of the studies agree that ten minutes will elicit that "better" effort athletes and coaches seek, and when the studies differ, they differ on the high and low ends of the ideal rest period. I have to chuckle a bit when I see cords being used forty minutes prior to a race at a meet; while this may provide a psychological boost (and in turn an increase in performance, as the placebo effect is certainly real), in my humble opinion (and the literature would say as much) the window of neuromuscular opportunity has long since closed. A psychological boost is good; a psychological boost combined with a true priming of the neuromuscular system is better.

2. Ten to twelve minutes is enough to provide a full recovery of creatine phosphate to the muscles, if needed, and this is obviously an important consideration for maximum performance in the sprints, where the "readiness" of the ATP-CP system is of primary focus. The recovery of the athletes prior to racing should be a top priority for coaches, and a benefit to training with PAP throughout a season is that the body is accustomed to this routine. Here at Liberty, our pre-race PAP routines are quite similar to Pure Power PAP practice sessions throughout the year, thus the body has been trained all season to replenish the ATP-CP system for race ready performances at our conference meet.

3. Ten to twelve minutes is also enough to recover mentally and emotionally from the PAP efforts; I do believe it would put unwelcome psychological stress on our women if we were to do PAP efforts three to five minutes prior to a 50 free, regardless of what the literature might say. We obviously do not want them in a rush five minutes before a race, worrying about their cap/goggle combination or having to run/walk quickly through a crowd on a slick deck to get to the ready room and so forth. Ten to twelve minutes

is plenty of time to relax, breathe, and walk confidently and purposefully to the staging area.

I should note the following regarding the mental side of the sport and, specifically, pre-race rituals: Our coaching staff here at Liberty believes in PAP, and the literature again would say as much; PAP works, and when used properly it can elicit faster performances in workouts and in meets. Our women also believe in PAP, and they have experienced firsthand and felt deeply the effects in workouts and in meet performances. They love it, and we want them to continue to love it and to believe in it, as we obviously want to continue to benefit from its use. A sure way to lose that belief is to, again, put unnecessary stress on the athletes too soon before a race or to have them feel as though PAP was to blame for a poor performance.

We do not want any stress other than the beneficial stress PAP elicits on the neuromuscular system, and a coach must pay careful attention to detail in this area of pre-race routines. If you lose that powerful belief due to a stressful and poorly planned pre-race PAP routine, it is extremely challenging to recover, especially with women. You absolutely do not want your athletes walking to the blocks with a doubt in their mind and thinking, *PAP doesn't work for me because that one time I felt slow*, and so forth. Make absolutely sure to get it right the first time and every subsequent time, for I am of the belief that a poorly planned pre-race PAP routine is more detrimental to fast swimming than no PAP at all.

While the neuromuscular benefit of a botched PAP session might still be there, waiting patiently to help unleash a fantastic performance, if the student-athlete is stressed out and unfocused walking to the blocks you certainly will not get the opportunity to see the neuromuscular benefit in action. For further reading into the power of the mind over the body and the importance of getting the PAP timing right, I highly recommend the book *Mind Over Mind* by Chris Berdik. It is a fascinating read into the realm of placebos, the power of belief, and a bit of neuroscience, and you will come away a better coach after having read this work, guaranteed.

We use cords as our primary PAP stimulus for meets, however our women also travel to meets with their personal parachutes, and they are free to use cords or chutes for their own specific pre-race ritual. Much of our specific PAP pre-race work is highly individual, as some of our women prefer the speed of assisted efforts with cords, while others enjoy the feeling of pulling on hard water with resisted cord efforts. Still others prefer resisted chute work, and some prefer a combination of the two or even all three. I will list some specific routines used by our women below:

Pre-Race PAP With Cords:

1 or 2 X 12.5 Max Blast resisted efforts against a cord or parachute with choice of gear

1 X 25 Assisted with a cord, no gear

1 X 25 Assisted with a cord, with no resisted efforts prior

1 or 2 X 12.5 Max Blast resisted efforts against a cord or a parachute with choice of gear, with no assisted effort to follow

. . . or any combination of the aforementioned efforts. Again, this is highly individual, as some of our women prefer resisted to assisted efforts and so on and so forth. With regards to the mental aspect of the pre-race ritual, if they believe in it, it is going to work, and as the literature tells us that both resisted and assisted efforts provide a PAP response, we let our athletes go with what they believe will work best for them.

We may also add some curveballs to the mix, so to speak, for example if we have an athlete who tends to slow into the turn, we may have them go the 25 cord assist to a foot touch, and in yet another example for fly and back types, we may go the 12.5s resisted against the cord all underwater body dolphin kick to make sure the legs are ready to rock and roll off the walls come race time. Jess Reinhardt went the following combo often at meets before the 100 fly and 200 medley relay:

Jake Shellenberger

2 X 12.5 Max Blast resisted against the cord with fins and paddles, 1 = kick, 2 = swim

1 X 25 Max Blast fly assisted with the cord, with no gear

This combination was fabulous to watch in action, as the 12.5 resisted kick and swim efforts against the cord elicited a major PAP response in the legs and arms that carried over to the 25 assisted effort, where she combined the leg action with the forced tempo of the cord to the arms.

In yet another example relating back to athletes who slow into wall for the turn, we have also experimented with not just assisted cords to a foot touch, but an assisted cord pull into a full turn, a push off, and then max dolphins off the wall into a two or four stroke breakout resisted against the same cord. This is a bit tricky to master for the coach administering said cord pull, but when it works, it is fun to watch and highly effective. The execution takes practice, but it can be perfected by both coach and athlete:

1. Start 10 yards from the wall, with athlete placing the cord in the middle of the back.
2. Athlete places the cord over the shoulder, with the hand holding the cord at head height so as to not put unnecessary stress on the shoulder when the cord is tightened.
3. Coach pulls the cord tight with athlete stationary, holding on to the lane line with the other hand.
4. When athlete can no longer hold on, she releases the cord and starts swimming toward the wall.
5. Coach pulls the athlete into the turn, easing up a bit into the turn, as we want to stay safe.
6. Athlete pushes off the wall as coach again pulls the cord tight.
7. Athlete explodes off the wall against resisted cord with race-specific number of turn underwater body dolphin kicks into the aforementioned breakout.

For a video demonstration of this technique, please visit the article on supplemental info for this book on my website at jakeshell.com.

Jake Shellenberger

PAP For Training

Moving on from the pre-race routines at competitions, again it is in the training, the day-to-day "getting after it," if you will, where I believe PAP can and does have the greatest benefit to increasing speed and ultimately performance in our sport, from 50 to 1650 types and everyone in-between. The possibilities for PAP training in workouts are limitless, and again, we are only restrained by our facilities, our creativity, and our athletes' bravery and willingness to go max, all-out efforts in practice.

Here at Liberty, we turn nearly every Pure Power swim and kick session into a PAP-based workout and quite often combine PAP work with Dive Max Quality efforts and Race Pace training. And why not, as the end goal is to swim faster; let us swim faster after our Pure Power efforts and put what the brain has learned into practice. When Rick DeMont would do PAP work on the Towers at Arizona, he would often say, "Okay, now let's put this into something that looks like fast swimming." The end goal, again, is always fast, natural, "free" swimming.

In the most basic example of PAP in workouts using the Power Tower, refer back to Chapter Two and the Post-Activation Potentiation example of Pure Power:

Six Rounds:
3 X 12.5

1 X 15

The 12.5s are Max Blast Swim @ 1:15 with fins, paddles, snorkel, bucket filled 50% on rounds one and two, 75% on rounds three and four, and 100% on rounds five and six. After each round of three 12.5 efforts on the Power Tower, we throw in a 15 Max Blast Swim with no Tower. Odd rounds in this example would be from a Push, even rounds from a Dive, choice flat or relay start, with the athletes using choice of gear on the push efforts.

The results are phenomenal, and those 15-meter Max Blast efforts with no Tower are some of the fastest 15s the athletes will ever swim. In fact, in many cases we are faster to 15 meters from a dive (timed from start to head at 15) in practice than we are in meets, even with using PAP as part

Jake Shellenberger

of our pre-race routine at said meets. Conference and NCAAs are a different story, of course, as a suit, shave, and rest are obviously at play.

I recall a specific example at Penn State with a young walk-on freshman named Ed Felty, and to this day it still remains the greatest example of PAP I have ever witnessed. The set was similar to the one above, going several rounds of:

2 X 12.5 Max Blast Swim

1 X 15 Max Blast Swim

Ed went the 12.5-yard efforts with a full Power Tower bucket, wearing fins, paddles, *and* five-pound ankle weights for an added PAP effect. The 15 was done with no gear whatsoever, and I submit to you today that the 15 push that Ed went after coming off the full bucket with ankle weights was *faster* than his 15 from a push on the second lap of his shaved, tapered, and suited 50 from that year. Perhaps it had to be seen to be believed, but it was cemented in my and Bill Dorenkott's minds as the greatest PAP effect we had ever seen.

Adding the ankle weights for a greater PAP effect is just scratching the surface in regards to ways coaches can "hack" this type of training, and, again, the creativity is limitless. Do you have resistance? Do you have a load that can be applied to the athlete in some way? Do you have a stimulus that will light up the neuromuscular system? Any of the above or combinations thereof can elicit a PAP response, and while I have not yet created a PAP effect in workouts greater than the one Ed Felty experienced all those years ago at PSU, we have come close here at Liberty, and I will share examples from our PAP training throughout this chapter.

I should note that "free" swimming and kicking are not the only components of our sport that can be trained using PAP techniques, as starts and turns are prime grounds for PAP work as well, and Rick hinted to as much with the quote that opened this chapter. On the following pages I will outline other forms of PAP training that we prescribe here at Liberty, and I will also share some of the dreams I have for PAP work, dreams that I cannot yet implement as I am limited by our facility in terms of space, equipment, and it being a REC operated pool. For coaches out there who have complete control over their facilities, I shall coach vicariously through you until we build our new facility here at Liberty!

Other Forms of PAP Work

Weight Belts

Sam Freas made weight belts quite popular through his *Sprinting* books, and we use weight belts often here at Liberty. As I will devote several pages to weight belts in the following chapter on other forms of resistance, I will only briefly discuss them here as they relate to specific PAP work. The use of weight belts is a fine candidate for PAP, and we use them primarily to elicit a PAP effect on starts and turns, but they can of course be used for free swimming as well.

Some sample weight-belt PAP sets:

Several Rounds:

2 X 15, 20, or 25 Dive Max Flat or Relay with an 8, 10, 12, 16, 20, or the heaviest 25-pound weight belt

1 X 15, 20, or 25 Dive Max Flat or Relay with no weight belt

Similar to the 12.5s Max on the Power Tower right into the 15 Max with no Tower, the aforementioned weight-belt dive efforts to no-weight-belt dive effort elicits a substantial PAP response. Stroke and kick tempos are increased, and time drops on the 15, 20, and 25 are enough to be seen with the naked eye, with the watch serving as a backup if necessary.

The effect is measurable and is twofold. First, we have a PAP response from the start, as we are loading the body similar to a weighted box jump, and the athletes fly off the block when they take off the weight belt. If you have ever had your athletes go weighted box jumps with a weight vest into a box jump with no weight vest you can attest; it is a marvelous sight to see elite athletes take off the weight vest and "jump through the roof" on the subsequent box jump with no weight. A similar effect occurs off the start when using weight belts in swimming, and especially with the 25-pound weight belt. If you want to see some *fast* relay starts, load up your athletes with a 25-pound weight belt, do a few relay starts, and then unload the belt. It is certainly fun to watch!

Secondly, the swim itself obviously produces a PAP effect, with the aforementioned stroke and kick tempo increased and the hips riding high in the water.

A quick note on the 25-pound weight belt:

We started with 5, 10, and 15-pound weight belts here at Liberty, then moved on to 20-pound weight vests (will cover in the next chapter), before deciding after five years of program history it was time to explore the true limits of weight-belt swimming. I will go into more detail in the next chapter, but for now, know that 25 pounds is not in fact, "too heavy" for elite athletes, and I am warming up to the belief that 25 pounds is not heavy enough.

Several Rounds (primarily as part of a power circuit):

2 X 20 High-speed turns with a heavy weight belt (again relative to the athlete)

1 X 20 High-speed turn with no weight belt

Weight belts are fantastic for training turns, as the athletes are forced to maintain their velocity into the wall, through the turn, and then off the wall into race-specific number of underwater body dolphin kicks into a breakout and swim. I have seen a few of our athletes try it, and I can tell you that it is nearly impossible to approach the wall, turn, push off, kick, and then breakout with anything less than all out maximal effort when using a heavy weight belt!

Coming off the belt, the turns are faster than the baseline. The approach, the turn, the push off, and the underwater body dolphins are sharper, cleaner, and a bit quicker after taking off the belt, and I am tempted to use weight-belt turns at our future conference meets as a pre-race PAP routine instead of cords, especially for those who tend slow into the wall (similar to cord assist to resisted turn).

Cords

Cords are our preferred method of inducing a PAP effect at meets, as they are easy to transport and can be used for resisted and assisted efforts. We use cords in workouts mainly for assisted work, as we believe that Power Towers, parachutes, and weight belts are far better for resisted efforts. We prescribe assisted efforts most often during power circuits or stations, with one or two 25-yard assisted sprints serving as a station in the power workout.

Some variations of cords that we use often:

1 X 25 Cord assist, going 12.5 under, 12.5 over

In this variation of a 25 cord assist, we'll have the athlete push off in a tight streamline position, holding the streamline for 12.5 yards with no kicking, then transition quickly into a perfect breakout at the 12.5 mark, followed by a 12.5 assisted swim. While this does limit the PAP effect of the assisted cord effort, we feel the added streamline and breakout practice is well worth the decrease in the PAP response.

1 X 25 Cord assist, underwater streamline

In this variation, the athlete simply holds a tight streamline position underwater with her partner pulling as fast as she can, stopping the pull at the flags as the athlete safely floats to the wall. While not PAP-inducing, this variation is great for practicing a tight streamline, as any inefficiencies in said streamline are magnified at cord speeds. If we have time leftover in a power station workout and want to have a bit of fun, we will hook two cords up to the athlete for double the pulling power, and with two cords she had better streamline . . . or else! Every once in a long while we will hook up three cords to an athlete and have three cord pullers; I recommend this only with highly experienced athletes, as the safety factor is certainly magnified with three cords pulling a streamline as fast as possible. While, again, not a PAP effect, this is fun for both athletes and coaches, and as Rick DeMont once said, "It is never a bad thing to go a 25 in eight seconds."

On a side note, Rick actually invented a machine at Arizona (along with the Power Tower) that pulls athletes in an assisted manner, using human power, over a 50-meter course. Using three pulleys, roughly seventy meters of rope, a belt, and some cords to aid in shock absorption, this pulling machine was a lot of fun to use and quite beneficial for the athletes. It was also beneficial for the lucky coach designated as the puller, for it was quite a good workout to pull athletes in an assisted manner over a 50-meter course. Imagine Prowler sled pushes for forty meters, and then add the resistance of an athlete moving through water, and you can get an idea. Along with filling up the Power Towers, pulling the Wildcats on the speed machine was another job of mine during my stay in Tucson, and I loved the challenge.

I should also mention the pulling efforts were all highly calculated and certainly not just random pulling as fast as I could. I would pull Roland Schoeman as close as I could to 21.7 for a 50 free, for example, and I actually had a stopwatch in my hand and timed him (with tempo) during his speed-machine-assisted efforts. I would pull the women at 24.5-25.5, with the idea that we wanted the brain to get a realistic feel for the physics of a body moving at 24.5 speed.

This leads me to another note:

When performing speed-assisted work, the goal should not be to pull the cord as fast as possible unless working on streamlining or having a bit of fun with three cords streamlining and so forth. There is a small pocket of track-and-field literature that speaks of assisted and downhill running, and the overwhelming consensus is that a window of up to ten percent faster than all-out maximum, race-competition speed is the upper limit when looking for neuromuscular adaptation. That is to say, anything faster than ten percent of an athlete's best effort will "confuse" the brain, and adaptations in the neuromuscular system will not occur. As the track folks tend to be a bit farther ahead than the swim community in regards to PAP research, I will take their lead and assume that we are also looking for the magical ten percent window.

I wrote about such a theory in my first book, *Letters to Chad: Building a Summer League Swim Team*, in which I recalled pulling 8-Unders on cords during my time as the head coach of the Mount Joy Summer Swim Team. It was the summer of 2006, and we had a chance to break the Lancaster

County Summer Swimming League record in the 8-Under girls' 100-meter free relay. I studied the track literature back then, and made sure to time each 25 assisted effort to make sure we were staying within the ten percent window. For example, our best 25-meter freestyler to start the summer went 18.0 at our "Blue/Gold Meet," and we pulled this athlete for quite a few 16.5 efforts during the remainder of the two-month summer season. At the championship meet, she was 16.2 in the relay, and the other three relay members showed similar drops. We went 1:11.50, breaking the existing league record by a wide margin. It is still the record, and while not extremely fast, it is decent for your average small-town summer league relay.

I was met with much resistance at the time (and not in a good, Power Tower kind of way) and still am today when I tell the story. "How could you pull eight-year-olds on cords?" they ask. "Weren't you worried about injury?" Again, it was all highly calculated, and looking back I find it funny that the same coaches who thought it ridiculous and unsafe to pull an eight-year-old on a cord had no problem throwing fins on them (a form of assisted work) and having them go sprint 25s at a speed faster than what I was pulling the cord.

Here at Liberty, we stay within the ten percent window or shoot for realistic competition goal times, and while we do not time every 25 assisted effort, we do time quite a few.

Two examples:

If a goal is 21.9 in the 50 free, we will want them out at least 10.6 to a foot touch in competition, and we estimate that would be 10.0 or so to a hand touch. In this realistic competition example of cord-assist training, we will then pull the athlete as close to 10.0 as possible for each assisted effort on the year. In a ten-percent-window example, suppose we have a goal of 22.80 in the 50 free, and we're looking to split 11.1 and 11.6 in that swim. We would estimate that she would be 10.6 to a hand touch, and we would look to pull no faster than 9.6 or so on assisted efforts throughout the year. Yes, it is more work to time assisted cord efforts, and it may come across as micromanaging to the athletes, but if assisted efforts outside of the ten percent window do not provide the stimulus needed by the neuromuscular system to produce adaptive changes, why do it? Yes, it may feel good to go that fast, but the risk of injury is increased, and the neuromuscular benefit may be reduced to simple entertainment for the athletes, at best.

Back to the Arizona speed machine: I took the concept back to Penn State, and as one can imagine, our engineers had a blast with the concept, building one for use in our 50-meter outdoor pool and achieving some mind-boggling results. For training streamlines specifically, we devised a way to hook up four belts and to pull the machine with four people, and you can achieve some serious speed with four college men running down a concrete deck in unison. No one believes me, but at our fastest we were able to pull a seven-second, 40-meter streamline, stopping well before the wall for obvious reasons. Imagine an underwater streamline at more than five meters per second—moving at that speed will certainly force an athlete to streamline properly, and my guess is that it would induce a flow state that is often quite rare in our sport.

In the summer here in Lynchburg, we simply attach two regular cords and use one long cord for 50-meter assisted work, whether swimming or streamlining. I do believe there is a benefit to 50-meter assisted work, as I believe it is a good thing for the brain to learn at high speeds in the big pool. DeMont said of the speed machine on July 25, 2007, "If you had to streamline 50 meters in ten seconds you're going to figure out some stuff, otherwise you're going to break parts of your body."

Medicine Balls

We have 20 and 30-pound medicine balls that we use here at Liberty for PAP work, and these are fantastic for eliciting a PAP response on starts and, to a lesser degree, on swim efforts. We used 5 to 8-pound med balls for PAP-related work when we started our program in 2010, but we did not move into the heavier range of medicine balls until this year. We plan on moving up to 40, 50, and even 60 pounds next year, as our strongest sprinters will have adapted to 20 and 30 over the course of this past year. We will have juniors and seniors next year who will be ready for such a weight, and I am exited to see the various PAP responses we can elicit from the heavier med balls. We have several exercises that we use for PAP work, and I will mention two here:

Med Balls for PAP Relay Starts as part of station or circuit power:

> 3 X Med Ball Relay Toss with 20 or 30-pound med ball (underhand med ball toss for distance . . . mimics a relay takeoff . . . emphasis on triple extension of hip, knee, and ankle and on throwing the arms forward explosively)
>
> 1 X 15 Dive Max from relay

In a variation, we might combine the med ball relay toss with a weight belt:

> 3 X Med Ball Relay Toss with 20 or 30-pound med ball
>
> 1 X 15 Dive Max from relay with a heavy weight belt
>
> 1 X 15 Dive Max with no weight belt, from relay

This variation produces some ultra-fast 15s, and it is fun to see the women flying off the block after taking off the weight belt. When I say fun, I mean these are some of the small moments that I love as a coach. Watching elite athletes on PAP-type work is a pleasure for me, as I am fascinated by human performance and potential. I would encourage you to practice a bit of mindfulness during your next workout and to try the following: stop, be completely in the moment, and thoroughly enjoy something specific about the current practice—a favorite athlete or something general about the sport. I try to do this at least once during every workout, and it has been a great exercise for me in mindfulness and gratitude. As for favorite athletes . . . Read the famous John Leonard article about favorites—yes, coaches certainly have them. No, that is not a bad thing, and I agree with Leonard here wholeheartedly.

The med ball relay toss with weight belt and relay-start PAP routine is an example with which I am limited (at least in the winter) by our facility, as ideally I would have the women on a concrete deck, taking an actual two-step relay approach for the med ball relay toss. As our tiled deck is slick, we do not want them moving their feet, and while we can still throw a pretty impressive standing underhand med ball toss for distance, I do believe we are missing out on not being able to move the feet as we would in a true relay start. I have an ideal solution that I will share a bit later in this chapter.

Medicine Balls for PAP - Flat Starts

While the medicine ball underhand relay toss is great for developing total body power and explosion and for closely mimicking the muscle action of a relay start, flat starts are certainly not forgotten and can also be trained for the aforementioned attributes using medicine balls; on a regular basis we implement both flat and relay-start medicine ball routines into our power workouts here at Liberty. We again use the same 20 and 30-pound loads, and as with the relay-start work, we will transition to heavier medicine balls next year. The flat start work with med balls is mainly geared toward the upper body, as weight belts work the lower body for flat starts better than a medicine ball.

Several Rounds:

3 X Med Ball Slams from overhead position

1 X 15 Dive Max, Flat Start

In this exercise, the athletes hold the medicine ball overhead, arms straight or with a slight bend in the elbow. Then, with a "high elbow catch," they slam the ball to the ground as quickly as possible. It is important to make sure the athletes are keeping their elbows high on the med ball, as this will allow them to throw it with more force and will mimic a proper stroking pattern in the water. This exercise is fantastic for teaching the athletes to incorporate the arms into the start, and we instruct them to pretend the edge of a block is a fourth med ball slam and to treat the block as if it were something to be thrown down and backwards forcefully. We believe in using the arms fully in the start here at Liberty, and while some coaches may disagree, we see nearly universal faster 15-meter times across the board when our women incorporate their arms more forcefully into the start and pull with a 100% 1RM-effort on the block.

In a variation of the previous routine, a whistle can be added to also help train reaction time, and we go roughly half of our med ball slams from a whistle "start," working reaction time, and half without.

Again, medicine balls can also be used for PAP swimming, and while we do not use this method often, I will share a set variation that we have used in the past and will most likely use again. If nothing else, it is something different for the women, and novelty is a good thing.

Med Balls for PAP - Swim Focus

Several Rounds:

2 X Med Ball Slams, with the 30-pound med ball

2 X 12.5 Max Blast Swim @ 1:15 on the Power Tower, with choice of paddles if any, no fins, bucket filled 1/2 to 3/4

Rest :45

2 X Med Ball Relay Toss with the 30-pound medicine ball

Rest :30 . . . Deep Focus . . . Deliberate Focus Mode

1 X 25 Dive Max from Relay take off to a foot touch, timed

If the goal is for a 22.8 freestyler to split 21.9 on a relay, we'll want her out 10.4 to a foot touch at the meet. Assuming a half second for a suit, shave, and taper and another tenth or two for the relay-start reaction time, we'll want her 11.0 or better from the feet leaving the block in practice.

In this set we have several PAP stimuli at work, with the med ball slams providing a bit of Post-Activation Potentiation for the Tower efforts and the Tower efforts then providing a stimulus for the 25 dive. The med ball relay toss efforts make sure the legs are not forgotten, and at the end of all of this, we see some *fast* 25s dive to the foot touch.

Again, we time from feet leaving the block, and the women are never 100% "to the wall" on the foot touch, so if you are comparing times, we are working with a perfect relay-start reaction of 0.00 and a 24.8-yard swim, but even so we have timed some fast 25s using this set in workouts, with quite a few 10.4, 10.5, and 10.6 efforts over the years, with our team record standing at 10.3. This is held by our 50-free school-record holder, Brye Ravettine, and would have put her relay start in the neighborhood of 21.3 had she ever anchored a relay (led off 200 free relay . . . backstroke on medley). As she was a 22.1 flat start 50, the 21.3 estimation is probably about right. We hesitate to estimate conference meet relay times from practice efforts, but if deciding on relay spots, a coach could use this type of set to gauge possible relay combinations.

Having written the previous section, I have decided to use this set and variations more often. As I recall, it did produce some fast swimming and is a fantastic total-body PAP experience.

Pull-ups for PAP work

We incorporated pull-up PAP work into our sprint training this year, and I believe it had a positive impact on our starts at our conference meet. While the concept is simple, coaching the student-athletes to fully incorporate what the brain is learning is a bit more complex. Deliberate, focused practice is key here, as I believe the specific PAP response we aim to see is lost if the athletes are not 100% dialed-in to the intent of the set.

Several Rounds:

3 X Pull-up, from a dead hang, from a varying whistle start, with 10-15 seconds rest between each pull-up

Right into:

1 X 15 Dive Max from a flat start

The goal is to train the brain to recruit as many motor units and muscle fibers in the arms and shoulders during the pull-up as possible, as quickly as possible. We combine this drill with a bit of visualization work, and the athletes are instructed before each pull-up to imagine themselves on the block, in lane four, in the final heat at the conference meet. "Look around," I tell them. "See the crowd. See the competition in other lanes. Hear the noise of your teammates cheering for you before the race. Step up on the blocks. Breathe deep. Relax. Now focus all of your energy, every last bit of energy, on your arms as you grip the block. On the whistle, you explode and rip the block with as much force as your arms and shoulders can summon. Rip the bar, rip the block, and explode up into the pull-up as fast as you can with as much power as is possible for you to generate. Take your mark . . ." Whistle! And they explode up into the pull-up.

They then walk to the block and after about thirty seconds of refocus and visualization go a flat start into a 15 dive max effort—the goal again is to "transfer" the pull-up into the start. We have seen some great results from this work and will continue to explore the potential. For an added bonus, a weight belt for the stronger athletes on the pull-up and the start can help elicit an even greater PAP response. An example:

2 X Weighted pull-up from a whistle start

Walk to the block, refocus

1 X 15 Dive Max with Weight Belt

Rest 1:00

1 X 15 Dive Max for time

In a real-world example of the this type of PAP work combined with Power Towers and med balls, the other day in practice we went the following set:

Eight Rounds:

1 X 15 Max Blast on the Power Tower, heaviest bucket possible, with fins and paddles

1 X Pull-up from a whistle start

1 X Med Ball slam from a whistle start

1 X 15 Dive Max, Flat Start

The amount of power and the rate-of-force development generated from the upper body on the 15 dive max was incredible, and several of our sprinters achieved lifetime best practice dive 15 times.

This type of routine is great for not only developing starting power, but also for seeing who has said power in the first place. Without any scientific experiments or research, I know instinctively through experience and from seeing thousands of starts and pull-ups that, on average, those who are better at the pull-up start routine on the previous page are also faster off the blocks. If I had been forward-thinking, perhaps I would have kept a running log for all the sprinters I coached, going back to the Penn State days, with two variables listed:

1. 15 Dive Max best time
2. 1RM Weighted pull-up

I am confident that the data would have been quite revealing! Perhaps someone out there has tracked similar metrics? My guess is that the sweet-spot combination of a stronger and more powerful athlete will hit the water at a maximum velocity higher than her weaker and less powerful opponent, all else being equal, more often than not, and will be faster to the 15 as a result. With regards to strength and starting power in general, if the reader is in the camp that believes swimmers should not strength train, simply consider the velocity at which an elite collegiate male sprinter leaves the block compared to an average or even above-average high-school female sprinter. Then consider the implications for the impact the sheer strength imbalance off the start will have for their respective 50 freestyle times, then, finally, revisit the concept of whether or not swimmers should strength train, especially women.

Taper Considerations

We continue our PAP training straight through our taper every year, for both our college and summer LCM seasons. This would make sense, as we will implement PAP at our conference and summer championship meets and do not want it to feel foreign to the body, to shock or fatigue the body in any significant way, or to negatively affect our psychological approach to each specific race. As PAP work closely mimics Pure Power work, refer to the taper considerations for Pure Power in Chapter Two for a refresher as to how we drop the Power Tower loads as we prepare for conference and summer championship meets.

While not as great, we still do see a PAP response from the lighter Tower loads during a rest, and we feel confident going into our championship meet that the neuromuscular system is right where it needs to be if we are still seeing a PAP response.

As noted in Chapter Two, this style of training can be extremely taxing on the neuromuscular system, perhaps more so when one considers the hacks that can be added to Pure Power work to produce a PAP effect. This type of training will also take a toll on in-season racing as the neuromuscular system is trained and strategically slightly over-trained, but again, I do believe the fatigue is worth the pain, as the drops are significant and the super compensation effects tremendous when rest is introduced and the neuromuscular system is allowed to fully recover. I believe a coach who implements PAP work throughout the season would be wise to err on the side of more and higher quality rest during a taper, especially when considering the 50 and 100 freestyle and 100 of stroke races. I have found that when thoroughly trained, the neuromuscular system does take a full three weeks to recover, and again, it is fun to see the "pop" return to the stroke as the rest accumulates throughout the taper.

With regards to rest and taper of the neuromuscular system as a whole, there are some who disagree that said neuromuscular system can be trained, believing instead that is "fixed," in a way, and that training it over the course a year and then over four years of a college career is a foolish if not impossible endeavor, rendering the above thoughts on taper for PAP work essentially useless. I would simply ask those of said belief to read the strength-training literature on the maximal-effort method and the neuromuscular adaptations that serious power lifters see over time. Either the neuromuscular system is changing and adapting or the weights are getting lighter; having known a few power lifters in my day, I can assure the reader they believe in training the neuromuscular system.

As it relates to swimming and specifically to sprint swimming, I have seen the adaptation and subsequent supercompensation/taper effect of the neuromuscular system at work, and I am not sure what else could account for the large time drops from in-season racing we have experienced here at Liberty. In short, the neuromuscular system, as it relates to PAP, can and should be trained fully over the course of a season and a four-year collegiate career.

Dreams of PAP

Medicine ball throws into relay starts and Power Towers into push and dive efforts are entry level in regards to what could be if coaches, athletes, and facility-management types were more willing to push the limits of the current norm. In one such example, I dream of the day when more pool decks are finished with running, jumping, and bumper plates in mind instead of the aesthetic value of tile. Certainly, we could find a cheaper alternative to tile where we could drop bumper plates, run, and jump with wet feet and worry little about falls or injuries in the process.

Imagine the type of PAP work and in/out of water combinations possible with such a setup. A dream of mine has always been a barbell with bumper plates on the pool deck, with swimmers in bare feet to maximize the brain's sensory perception and awareness with the ground—we do relay starts with bare feet, after all. I believe our hang cleans should follow the same rationale.

Just a few of the many visions I have:

2 X Heavy Hang Clean

Quick 30-second refocus

1 x 15 or 20 or 25 Running Dive Max

2 X Heavy Hang Clean

Quick 30-second refocus

1 x 15 Dive Max from Relay Start

2 X Heavy Hang Clean

Quick 30-Second Refocus

1 X 12.5 Max Blast Swim Power Tower with a HEAVY bucket

Quick 30 Second Refocus

1 X Pick something fast . . . 15 Dive Max, 25 Dive Max to a Foot Touch, 15 Running Dive, Run down the pool deck and dive into a high speed turn, etc.

2 X Heavy Hang Clean

Quick 30 Second Refocus

1 X 25 Dive Max with weight belt, flat or relay

1 X 25 Dive Max no weight belt, same flat or relay as above

And so on and so forth. All of these exercises can also be combined with a whistle start, as with the previous pull-up example, and I would love to see more Olympic lifts, or otherwise, performed to whistle starts, both in the weight room and on the pool deck. An example:

Jake Shellenberger

3 X Heavy Trap Bar Deadlift or Hang Clean from a whistle start, following the same visualization protocol from the pull-ups example, with plenty of rest between each effort

Quick 30-second refocus

1 x 15 Dive Max—transfer the lift into the start, Roland Schoeman style!

The possibilities are limitless if one had a surface where barbells with bumper plates could be thrown at will. Brushed concrete decks have gone in and out of style in recent years, and my hope is that they make a comeback, and for good. Just two of the many downfalls of tile are the inability to throw weight, if desired, and the lack of traction with bare feet and, in some cases, shoes. If you were at the women's NCAAs at Auburn in 2012, you will remember the epitome of a slippery deck. Blue mats were thrown down en masse to protect the athletes and coaches from falling, but still the tile (and mats) tallied quite a few victims that weekend. Also in 2012, at our CCSA championships, one of our own Liberty student-athletes slipped on the tiled deck and broke her wrist during the second day of the competition. The injury knocked her out of the meet and led to her eventual retirement; I believe she would have stayed in the sport had she not broken her wrist. It is quite sad to think we've been trading aesthetics for safety and athletic performance when it comes to pool decks over the years!

I have the unique and rare opportunity here at Liberty to design our new pool as I wish (within the budget of course), from scratch. You had better believe a brushed-finish concrete deck is on the non-negotiable list, and as long as I am coaching here, it will not be tiled.

Thoughts on traction and slipping aside, in regards to PAP work and the deck finish: Concrete is fantastic for athletic movements, and with some rubber matting can handle bumper plates without cracking. Hang cleans into racing efforts with Power Towers and weight belts are just a glimpse into what the collective creative power of coaches could and would unleash if the deck provided the opportunity. I am excited to see the outcome as more and more pools (hopefully) go back to deep-brushed concrete decks.

Dumbbell work can also be incorporated into PAP training, and one can substitute dumbbells for the various barbell exercises I listed above. Again, the possibilities are endless. Perhaps dumbbell rows into racing efforts or various dumbbell overhead lifts into racing efforts and so forth can be prescribed.

Having mentioned barbells, bumper plates, and concrete decks, I concede that, yes, the more affluent programs could simply buy Olympic lifting platforms for their tiled pool decks, but good luck finding a REC aquatics director who will allow said platforms as a mainstay on their deck. And for meets, what then? Concrete is the way to go, and I urge anyone reading this work with influence in the aquatics design/construction industry to urge the building of more concrete decks. What we will lack in aesthetic value we will more than make up for with increased safety and multiple options for in/out of water training, dryland, and athletic movements.

In closing, PAP work goes far beyond cord pulls at meets, and this is an area where the creativity of our coaching body could make huge improvements in training, and in sprint training in particular. I dream of the days following the completion of our facility, when I am free to incorporate the visions described in the preceding pages. Imagine walking into a sprint practice here at Liberty and seeing athletes in the near purest form—with just a suit on—using various Olympic lifts and other movements to elicit PAP responses in their training. Heavy trap bar deadlifts into racing efforts, cleans into Power Tower efforts, and the list goes on and on. Perhaps a two-hour power practice also doubles as a strength-training session, and our strength coach is on deck with us—now we have double the creativity working together to train our women, and we would also save an hour from our NCAA-regulated CARA limits. Can you see it? Can you envision a two-hour power session combining barbells, plates, Power Towers, weight belts, music, etc., all right there on the pool deck, with one current and one former C.S.C.S.-turned-swim-coach working together to push the limits of the collective cognitive creative of our sport? It will happen, and it will happen in 2017 here at Liberty.

I would like to consider myself a creative mind, though I have no doubt the reading of this section will spur you to find new and better ways than what I have described in this chapter to use PAP in your workouts. We know from the literature that PAP work does in fact elicit a faster effort post-catalyst, and the possibilities are limitless with regards to the training combinations that the most creative coaches and athletes can achieve. The future of Post-Activation Potentiation mixed sprint training is exciting, to say the least!

Jake Shellenberger

Chapter 8: Other Forms of Power & Resistance

"de Bruijn, Ja! Ja! Ja! Ja!"

Dutch TV announcer after Inge de Bruijn wins gold in the 50 free in Athens, 2004

WHILE I have dealt mainly with the Power Tower thus far, this work would be incomplete if I did not also mention other forms of power and resistance training that we use here at Liberty and that saw action during my time at Penn State and Arizona. As is no surprise, Power Towers are my favorite form of resistance training for the various reasons stated in the preceding seven chapters. However, the devices on the following list alsohave many benefits. We use the term "toys" here at Liberty to describe said devices, and there are many workouts where we give our women the autonomy to use whatever toys they think will help them the most on that particular day and set. As we know, perception is reality, and if they believe it is what is best for them in the moment, it is hard to debate otherwise!

As for the *why* in regards to the variety of toys we use, among several reasons I will list two specifically. First and foremost, novelty is something rare in the swimming world, and as much fun as Power Towers are (for me at least), if they were our only form of resistance training, I do believe even the mighty Towers would become mundane and would lose their appeal, even to our most dedicated and enthusiastic sprint types. The brain is fascinating in this regard; it loves the day-to-day habits and rituals that allow it to conserve precious cognitive horsepower, but the excitement of the novel is certainly a motivator and elicits a strong dopamine response. Novelty in training is a good thing, and we are sure to adhere to this rule with our power training here at Liberty.

Secondly, while I believe in the principle of specificity, I also believe in the benefits of GPP, or general physical preparation, as it is known in the strength and conditioning world, and I believe adamantly that water-resistance training should be varied as much as possible without losing the specificity that fast swimming requires. This is perhaps a throwback to my strength and conditioning days, as many of the top strength coaches in the country put a high value on variety in their programs. As per one small example, a resisted Power Tower effort will provide a somewhat even resistance throughout the swim, while a resisted cord effort will increase in resistance the farther the athlete moves from the cord anchor point. One is not necessarily better or worse than the other; it depends on the goal of the specific set and on the desired outcome of the training session as a whole.

The many toys, then, allow a total-body, varied approach to power and sprint training, and while at the end of the day we are drag cars moving in straight lines, a general, wide base of power training in its various forms provides what I believe is a higher ceiling for the more specific Power Tower training outlined in the preceding chapters.

Power Rack

As I covered the advantages and disadvantages of Power Towers versus Power Racks at length in Chapter Two, I will not go in depth here. To summarize, the Power Rack is great for programs on a strict budget and for Pure Power work, but on the whole I would suggest the use of Towers over Racks.

Drag Sox

Drag Sox are an interesting power-training device from Aqua Volo out of California, and we have a pair for each of our student-athletes here at Liberty. In short, the Drag Sox are a smaller version of a mesh training bag that covers the feet and provides quite a bit of resistance when kicking and full stroke swimming. We use them often, and they are a frequent choice when our women are given the option of "C.O.T." (choice of toys) on various Pure Power kick and swim sets. While they are a popular choice for 12.5s, it is funny to see how little they are used when the distance is stretched to a 15, and fewer still choose them when we go 25s for Power Endurance-type work. We use the largest, hardest size—60—and, yes, it is quite a challenge to stay max when the distance is increased to anything over 15.

Drag Sox can be used for both kicking and swimming for Pure Power, Power Endurance, and drilling sets. Similar to the anti-paddle, I like the idea of taking away the feeling of water on the feet and then bringing it back again, and I believe this is an area where athletes can make great improvements in their kick. We talk often about feeling water and improving sensory perception of the hands when we swim . . . if only our athletes would put as much focus and emphasis on feeling that same water with the feet! Drag Sox force this adaptation on the brain, and you can "see" it when they come off the Sox into regular kicking or swimming. For example, a sprint freestyler might go several rounds of:

> 3 X 12.5 Max Blast Underwater Dolphin Kick with Drag Sox
>
> 1 X 15 Max Blast Kick no Drag Sox, going race specific number of dolphins off the wall, with a transition to MAX free kick on the surface in a tight streamline to finish out the kick

Again, you can see the feet grabbing more water on the 15, and I believe the brain is making neural and sensory adaptations along the way.

For an added bonus, some of our stronger women might go the previous set with the Drag Sox efforts on the Power Tower, and in still another example, we might add weight belts to the mix. Kicking on a Power Tower with no fins is tough; kicking on a Power Tower with no fins and with 60-weight Drag Sox is quite the challenge, indeed!

As mentioned, Drag Sox can also be used for Power Endurance work and for both kicking and swimming. Sub-maximal but *fast* 25-yard swim and kick efforts work well for this training, and it is not uncommon to see our distance types swimming repeat 25s with Drag Sox and paddles to work Power Endurance. The creativity is limitless—anything you prescribe for a normal set can be magnified with Drag Sox for an added resistance benefit. In one such example, we added Drag Sox to a dive quality set (much to the dismay of some of our women):

> 8 X 50 Dive Max @ 4:00, broken at the 25, going:
>
> 25 Dive Max with Drag Sox to a foot touch
>
> Remove Drag Sox, Rest 5 seconds
>
> Push 25 Max breathing once or none on the way home

This was a tough set, and the women were forced to power through their underwater body dolphins and breakout off the start with an effort that might be hard to summon otherwise.

Drag Sox are also great for drilling, and in one example we use them with the Zona Drill I described in previous chapters. The drill:

> 12 X 50 As:
>
> 4 X 50 With paddle on right hand, fin on left foot, and Drag Sox on right foot
>
> 4 X 50 With paddle on left hand, fin on right foot, and Drag Sox on left foot
>
> 4 X 50 With fins and paddles on both hands and feet

The 4 X 50 at the end looked fantastic, effortless perhaps, and we saw times on a watch that were unexpected, considering it was a drill set and the women were not instructed to go fast. They felt so good in the water, however, that speed was a natural byproduct without them trying to go fast.

Aqua Volo Kick Bands

The Aqua Volo Kick Bands are oversized rubber bands that fit around the ankles when kicking free or back, and, similarly to Drag Sox, they provide resistance on the up and down beat of the kick. As an added bonus, the band size can be changed, and some of our stronger women throughout our program's history have kicked quite well with a smaller size band. Yet another added bonus: On a small setting, these bands do a great job of keeping the kick inside the body cylinder, obviously important for fast free and backstroke kicking.

We do not use these bands as often as our other toys, but they do provide a good amount of resistance, and we will keep them in our equipment bag for as long as Aqua Volo produces them.

Weight Belts

Where to begin with weight belts? I have grown to love them over the years, and in writing this book, I was tempted to dedicate an entire chapter to weight belts alone. In the end, common sense won out; while this specific section on weight belts is exhaustive, a separate chapter all together might be just a bit too much.

I was first introduced to the idea of weight belts in 2002 by Sam Freas and his original 1995 *Sprinting: A Coaches Challenge* book, then firsthand at Penn State in 2006. My first impression was that I was not all that impressed.

We used five and ten-pound belts with our sprint crew, and looking back, while great for endurance training, I do not believe the belts were heavy enough to elicit the type of adaptations and "wow factor" for sprinting that I see with them today. Wearing multiple belts became bulky and awkward, and the PAP response Bill Dorenkott and I saw was little to nonexistent, even for our women. With Power Towers providing a much greater (and certainly more exciting) response, we spent the majority of our time with Towers. Freas recommended two to ten-pound belts in his original book, and knowing what I know now about the belts and the beginnings of their ceiling/limits, of course five and ten pounds were much too light for a true PAP response, especially for our top sprint men. The women showed a greater neuromuscular response from the ten-pound belts, but even then I was still not overly impressed.

We had some strong sprinters in that Penn State group, with men who could pull two full Power Tower buckets a full 25 in under 13 seconds and women who could pull a full bucket for a 25 under 14. Men with 400-pound deadlift max efforts and women max squatting 250 and so forth were commonplace, and, while obviously nothing to write home about in the power-lifting world, a 400-pound deadlift max for a male swimmer is impressive, in my humble opinion. A ten-pound weight belt or even two of them simply will not go far in eliciting a PAP response for a 6'4" 230-pound South African male sprinter.

Note: The five and ten-pound belts were, again, great for endurance work, and I have no doubt that our mid-distance and distance crews at PSU benefitted greatly from their use. My thoughts above deal with sprinting and specifically the PAP response (and lack thereof).

Looking back, I don't know why we never thought to buy heavier belts— perhaps we were unsure of their worth in training, or we were simply following the accepted protocol of other coaches. At any rate, I was not immediately convinced of the true value of weight belts while at PSU, even though they came highly recommended from Freas as far back as 1995 and from Cecil Colwin in his 2002 classic, *Breakthrough Swimming*, which I read many times during my days in Happy Valley.

As a coach, I discovered, quite by accident, that by wearing a weight belt most swimmers will automatically exert maximum leverage on the water and, in the process, find the stroke pattern best suited to his or her own body build or, to phrase it colloquially, his or her own individual set of levers. (Colwin 2002, 47)

When I moved to Virginia to start our program here at Liberty in 2009, weight belts were on the list of training aids to buy (though I was sure to acquire three Power Towers first), and again I went with five and ten-pound belts. As noted, I did use them at Penn State; it was not that I thought they were an unnecessary, I simply was not convinced they were as good as Freas made them out to be. I did not prescribe them more than one to two times a week and often went a week or two without prescribing them at all. They were a treat, perhaps, not a staple in our sprint diet at PSU.

The same five and ten-pound weight-belt protocol lasted until 2014, here at LU, but changed drastically late in that season when, during a power workout, I asked one of our stronger sprint women if she would like to try wearing two ten-pound weight belts. I enjoy exploring the athletes' individual limits a bit when it comes to sprint training and resistance/power work, and she was more than excited for the challenge. The set was a mixture of 15s and 12.5s Max Blast using both Power Towers and weight belts, and her neuromuscular system was primed and ready for the task.

For a warm up, we went:

1 X 15 Max Blast Swim with a ten and five-pound belt for 15 total with fins and paddles

Then, after a minute of rest:

1 X 15 Max Blast Swim with two ten-pound belts with no gear

Again, this young woman was quite strong, with a 185-pound hang clean max and a squat max of 230, and she was a junior at the time with almost three full years of experience in our program and two full summers behind her. I certainly would not have asked a freshman to attempt such a task, and I should also note she was a 22+ 50 type and 49 in the 100. To my surprise, it was actually quite easy for her, and it did not look much different than a normal 15 max effort without a weight belt. Her hips were a bit lower than normal in the water, sure, but not substantially lower, and nothing about the mechanics of the swim told me subconsciously or intuitively that she was at risk of injury due to a radically altered stroke technique.

Those of you who have spent 10,000 hours in the weight room can relate—after that long, you instinctively know when someone's back or knees are not in the correct anatomical position to squat or deadlift safely and so forth. While the differences in incorrect versus correct weight-room technique are subtle, and vary by athlete, the brain of a master can spot them, even if below the level of conscious thought and awareness (See *Outliers* by Malcom Gladwell and the Greek statue story for more).

In short, for the previous eight years I had not prescribed any heavier than ten pounds for a weight belt because of one reason—intellectual inertia. Ten pounds was the heaviest individual belt we used at Penn State, and ten pounds was the heaviest that Sam Freas recommended, and thus ten is what we used for the first four years of program history here at Liberty. What we did was what we had always done, and while it seems silly to look back now and wonder why I never bothered to try more weight, when you are in the moment and living the day to day, you can easily lose the ability to experiment with something as simple as a heavier belt. We used multiple belts on rare occasions at PSU, and, again, it was awkward to wear more than one. I believe subconsciously I shut myself off from the idea of more weight due to that experience, and it took the aforementioned *Ah hah!* moment here at Liberty to shake myself free.

On a side note, it pains me to imagine the amount of breakthroughs and innovations in sport, business, academia, and otherwise that we might be missing due to this phenomenon, and thankfully the idea to try twenty pounds popped into my head, and we had an athlete willing to try the experiment. In what areas of your program might you be experiencing intellectual inertia? Sometimes a quick stop and exhale allows us the time to take stock of our thought processes and measure them against this concept. Do we do it the way we have always done it because it is better . . . or because we are stuck in perpetual cognitive motion?

After the ease of the twenty-pound effort and the release of Sam's second book, *Sprinting II: It Takes Guts*, in which he now recommended four to sixteen-pound belts, I knew we were ready and willing to go with heavier loads. The rest, as they say, is history. It took two years and a bit of equipment budget manipulation, but we now have over twenty Watermark Pro weight belts, ranging in weight from six to twenty-five pounds, and we plan to buy more. We use them three to four times per week, for all training groups, and I am excited to see the short and long-term effects over the course of a season and training career, as our women adapt and move from lighter to heavier belts.

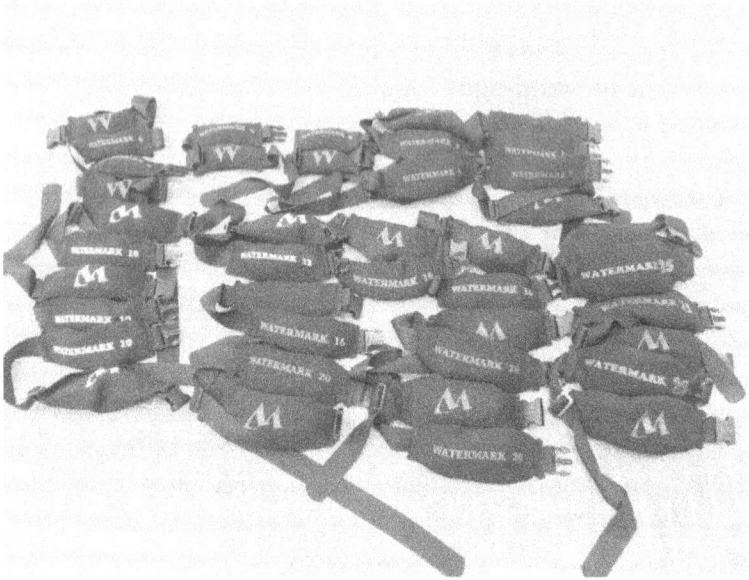

A quick story about the twenty-five-pound belts, of which we have three: Upon attempting to purchase a twenty-five, thirty, and thirty-five-pound belt, I was simply told no; that is to say, the company (who will remain nameless) we chose to buy from would not sell us the belts. I was told these were extremely heavy, that they were dangerous, and that they were only for "elite programs and athletes." At this point in five years of program history, we had qualified five different athletes and a relay to the NCAA DI championship meet in three of those five seasons, scoring points twice. With those NCAA qualifiers setting program records of 51.72 in the 100 fly, 1:00.01 in the 100 breast, and 22.19 in the 50 free, I wondered to myself what exactly it meant to be an elite program or to have elite athletes? Stanford and Cal we certainly were not, but considering our infancy and humble beginnings, I thought we had come far in just five years.

Remembering how easy the twenty-pound belt was and guessing that not many of the "elite" programs feature women with 185-pound hang clean efforts, I knew we could handle the weight.

Cooler heads prevailed, and eventually we were "allowed" to purchase one twenty-five-pound belt to test out after I convinced the good folks that, yes, although I realized they had never heard of Liberty, I could guarantee that we did have elite athletes here and we could handle the twenty-five-pound belt. If things went well, we were told, we could buy more, and, yes, things went well indeed.

We now have three twenty-five-pound belts, as I mentioned, and have since started a competition and are keeping track of team/personal records in a:

Dive 25 Max

To a hand touch

With a 25-pound belt

No gear

From a block with a track plate

Jake Shellenberger

Thus far, our fastest effort has been 13.09 from a 22.6/49.0 sprint free-styler—if anyone out there has a twenty-five-pound belt, or is thinking of buying one, and wants to compare.

While the twenty-five-pound belt is heavy, yes, the feat has been at-tempted and completed by half of our team, from sprint types to distance swimmers alike. All have completed the effort with good technique, and in times that I believe are quite fast considering the weight of the belt, ranging from the aforementioned 13.09 to a 14.74. If you take a random adult male off the street and ask him to dive a 25 max with no weight belt, he will have a hard time going 13 seconds, and that is what our sprint types can do with a twenty-five-pound weight belt strapped to their hips. It's heavy, yes, but it's nowhere near muscular failure, as compared to a lift in the weight room, and nowhere near creating a degradation in tech-nique to the point where I fear for the safety of the women. In my humble opinion, twenty-five pounds is only scratching the surface of what is pos-sible with a weight belt, and had I listened to the good folks who sold us the belts, I would have thought this weight impossible for college women not swimming at an "elite" program.

I will go so far as to say that twenty-five pounds is light for elite athletes, and 13.09 is just the beginning, with regards to our weight belt challenge. Unfortunately, the three school-record holders I mentioned earlier all graduated before they could attempt this feat, and remembering how strong they were in the weight room and their abilities to go full bucket Power Towers easily and so forth . . . I have no doubt that all three of them would have been faster than our current 13.09 record. Though not an individual school-record holder, the young woman with the 185-pound hang clean max who went the twenty-pound belt with ease would have also been under.

Weight Belt General Thoughts

Weight belts fascinate me, and after the twenty-pound breakthrough two years ago and increasing our arsenal since then, I can now see why Sam Freas believes in the belts as much as he does. I have spent much of the past year attempting to understand what exactly is happening when an athlete attaches one to the hips and sprints at a maximal effort. Of the many intellectual interests I have in life, at the risk of sounding silly, I must

Jake Shellenberger

admit that the physics, physiology, and psychology of training with Power Towers and weight belts in our sport ranks quite high on the list.

As we know, swimming is a cerebral sport, and while I could be biased, of the various coaching professions, I consider swimming to be one of the most intellectually demanding in nature. Consider that, at the baseline level, at the minimum, a working knowledge of the aforementioned physics, physiology, and psychology are molded by average to good coaches to produce fast swimming. At the highest level, the majority of coaches who have achieved mastery and consistently produce elite-level athletes have developed a deep understanding of at least these three cognitive disciplines, and probably more. These masters might stretch their depth even further in the area of physics; for example, they might consider the complications arising in the sub-disciplines of hydrodynamics and human biomechanics as they observe a body moving through the water.

What, then, can we determine from wearing weight belts when swimming? What is happening to the body, and what forces are at work? Why do weight belts work? How do they affect technique, and are the changes for better or for worse? How do they increase strength and power? Do we know they actually work, or are we just taking Sam Freas, Cecil Colwin, myself, and a few other coaches at their words? Have we adequately tracked the metrics of weight-belt training? Can we be sure said metrics are accurate and that the belts produce positive physiological changes? Back to Colwin, who certainly shares the intellectual approach to coaching:

> Freestyle swimmers find that wearing a weight belt has a positive effect on their ability to place the stroke exactly where the strongest leverage results. The freestyle swimmer automatically adjusts the entry point of the hands to a position where he or she naturally feels the strongest resistance of water during the pull, even after the weight belt is removed. (Colwin 2002, 47)

Colwin is on to something here, and in a way, is describing Post-Activation Potentiation when speaking of the weight belt being removed, perhaps without realizing it. Weight belts are quite the physics challenge, indeed! From my experience, I would agree with Colwin in regards to stroke placement and leverage, and I believe we see this same phenomenon in the heavy Power Tower efforts described throughout this book. The athletes enter with fingertips down with the hand, wrist, and forearm achieving the EVF sooner than in unresisted stroking because they simply must; if the athletes are not providing a backwards propulsive drag force early in the stroke, they will lose forward momentum, at the least, and cease forward velocity or go backwards, at worst. I believe the brain can feel this, and thus the athletes instinctively get to the EVF more quickly or "automatically" achieve this position, as Colin states.

I do have questions as to exactly what leverage is being used when we swim with the weight belt and then comparing the belt versus the Power Tower. I wonder of the physiological training adaptations and stroke changes the two training devices produce. What exactly is happening from physiological and technical perspectives? I have always been a believer that the drag propulsion force is the primary mover in fast swimming, not lift force, as was the generally accepted theory in the 1970s and 80s, with a few believers of lift force still entrenched today, particularly in regards to the sculling action in breaststroke. I believe that both forces contribute to fast swimming in all four strokes, with a focus on the front-to-back, straight-line application of drag force as the greater of the two (even with breaststroke, we teach a more north-to-south pull here at Liberty, not a true scull stroke). How, then, does a weight belt play into the push/pull of lift versus drag force? What are the training considerations?

A Power Tower provides a somewhat simple example of the front-to-back, straight-line drag force in action; the Tower provides a relatively straight line of nearly horizontal resistance, and the swimmer must counter said resistance with her own drag propulsion in a north-to-south, straight-line pull. I prefer the Tower for this reason, as it teaches this north-to-south pull perhaps better than any other drill or training device I have seen or used. The weight belt, on the other hand, challenges the athlete with a downward vertical resistance, and at first glance it would appear that lift force and the S-shaped pulling pattern would play a greater role in propulsion with a weight belt than would the drag force. But does it?

Much research has been done since Councilman popularized the idea of lift force as the primary propulsive force in swimming in the 1970s, and the consensus from said research is that drag force propulsion is the more important of the two. Dr. Brent Rushall, of USRPT fame, is one of the foremost proponents of drag force, and I would encourage a visit to his site to learn more. This is an area in which I agree with him wholeheartedly. As the lift force acts perpendicular to the flow of the body and hands through water, I would assume that increasing the speed at which said body and hands move through the water would in turn increase the lift force, allowing the swimmer to overcome the vertical resistance of the weight belt. While lift force is not always strictly counteracting a vertical resistance, in the case of a swimmer moving horizontally through the water in a nearly straight line, with her hands ideally doing the same, I believe we can say with some certainty that in swimming, an increased velocity and in turn, a greater lift force would counteract a vertical, downward force.

In perhaps a more practical example, we know that the body rides low in the water when athletes swim slowly; when the velocity is increased the body and hips naturally ride higher, and this is the lift force at work. More research on weight belts, specifically, and on their affect on biomechanics and swimming technique is needed. We have a bit of research on resisted swimming, but I could not find any research on weight belts, specifically, and I would love to see exactly what is happening from biomechanical and physiological standpoints.

Weight Belt Benefits

Without any formal research, my eyes, my general observations, my personal theories, and feedback from our athletes tell me of several major benefits to training with weight belts, and I will outline just a few of many on the following pages.

Increased Core Strength & Endurance

I believe regular use of weight belts in training strengthens the core, and for these purposes, I would determine the core to be from the upper chest to the knees. I see a body moving through the water horizontally as a bridge, with the core as the span and the hands and feet (with their subsequent leverage, as Colwin would say) acting as the piers that support the span. While not a perfect analogy, I believe this works well for the purposes of understanding the benefits of a weight belt in training. The belt then acts as a load on the span, and the span must support the weight of the belt through increased strength, endurance, and neuromuscular connectivity with the piers. While not perfect, a resisted core bridge or plank in the weight room is nearly the land equivalent, with the arms and feet acting as the piers supporting the body or span.

The challenge, of course, in the pool is that water is much harder to anchor against than an immovable floor or the ground, and thus, while wearing the weight belt, the athletes must attempt to anchor the piers of their bridge against a surface that is constantly in motion. Here at Liberty, we talk about finding "hard water" in/on which to anchor the hands, and for our sprinters, we teach a deep, north-to-south, straight-line pull that attempts to find said water. This is not easy, of course, but try it, and I do believe your athletes will find the leverage that Colwin describes above.

Imagine a body moving through the water in the photographs on the next page. As seen in the marked-up photos on the subsequent pages, the athlete's hands and feet act as the piers, and the core must support the load and the span through said piers. I am not a structural engineer, nor do I have an advanced degree in human biomechanics, but I believe it a good thing to train these positions with resistance.

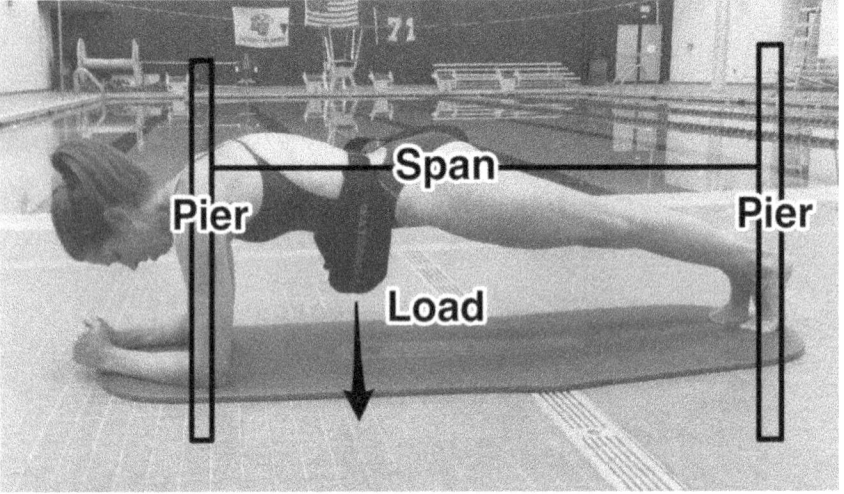

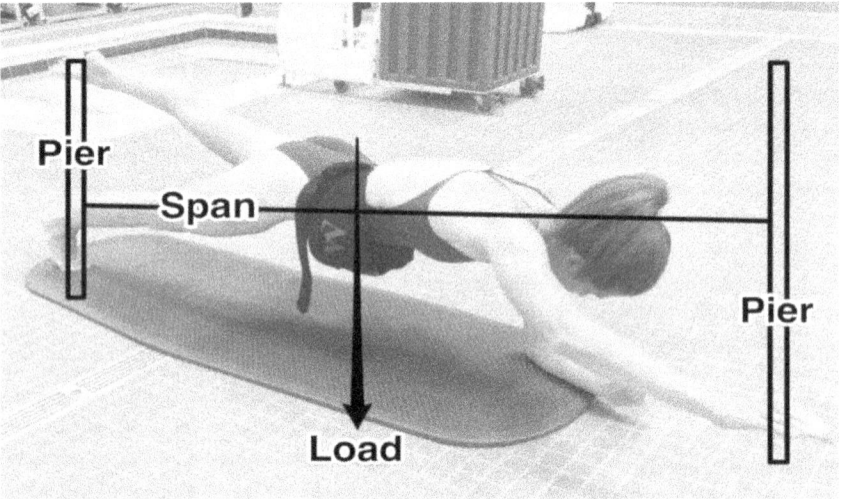

While not weighted, the ab wheel device gives us another land exercise that mimics the effects of weight belts in training, and the athletes must engage the core with all the strength and endurance they have in order to support the body at the base of the ab wheel position.

I see the weight belt, then, as combining a weighted core bridge with swimming, working the span strength and endurance with the pier connection in a way that adheres to the much discussed, and often obsessed over, principle of specificity in training. Perhaps a logical progression would be to:

1. Train core strength and endurance through resisted bridges in the weight room

2. "Transfer" the gained core strength and endurance to specific in-water adaptations with the weight belt

3. Finish with unresisted "free" swimming

This progression could be trained in the acute and chronic sense of the term, with the above three steps trained over the course of a career and in individual training sessions as the athletes adapt to increased loads. Perhaps one might go a set in a specific workout of:

Several rounds of:

3 X 30 Second medium weighted core bridges on the pool deck, resting 15 seconds between efforts

3 X 50 @ :60 with a light weight belt, at 80% of max effort, with a focus on span/pier engagement and keeping the hips high in the water

Rest 30 seconds

1 X 50 at 96% effort, with no weight belt, focusing again on span/pier engagement and *fast* but not max effort "free" swimming

A sprint example:

Several Rounds of:

3 X 20 Second heavy weighted core bridges on the pool deck, resting 20 seconds between efforts

3 X 15 Max Blast with a heavy weight belt—engage the span/piers!

Rest 30-60 seconds

1 X 25 Dive Max or 1 X 15 Push Max

Feedback from the athletes is important here, as you want to make sure they are thinking about and focusing deliberately on engaging the core and doing everything in their power to swim with adequate technique and body position. I say adequate because, as with the Power Towers, I believe that a training device that causes a change in body position, as the weight belt can do, is okay if the device has more benefits than the negatives associated with the change in position. For example, while yes, the weight belt causes a change in body position with lower than normal "free swimming" hips, if we are strengthening the core and pier connectivity, I believe we have a net gain benefit on the back end. The principle of specificity purists would disagree, stating that because a weight belt changes the body position in the water and changes the stroke technique, it should not be used because the body position is not 100% specific to racing conditions. It is here where I part with the purists for the aforementioned reasons, and the reader can refer back to Chapter Three on Pure Power for more thoughts regarding the principle of specificity in training and why I believe we over-emphasize the importance of this training concept.

As for the feedback, if you are going to implement weight belts in your program, you need to constantly solicit feedback from your athletes to make sure they are deliberately engaging the core and pier connection while swimming. Just one of many examples, this one is from a workout two weeks ago, and I paraphrase:

Jake Shellenberger

Me: "Where did you feel the weight belt today? What did you learn?"

Athlete A: "I felt it in my core. I had to flex my abs to keep my hips up for the entire 50."

Athlete B: "It hurt my lower back a bit. It was hard."

Both of these athletes have similar strength levels in the weight room, and both have similar times and abilities in the pool. Both were using the same six-pound weight belt for a set of 50s, during which the goal was to work core endurance. (The six-pound belt is extremely light.) From this feedback, I gathered that Athlete A was, of course, using the weight belt correctly, focusing on span/pier engagement with a deliberate, focused effort on each 50 to keep her hips riding high on the water. Athlete B may have lost focus a bit and allowed the hips to sink, causing a "sag" in her span and putting unnecessary pressure on her lower back. Picture the weighted core bridge again in the weight room—Athlete A was focusing on maintaining a horizontal plane or even holding the hips higher than the head/feet, while Athlete B would be the one you walk past and readjust the hips because they were too low.

Athlete B was, then, of course instructed to focus more on the hips and span/pier engagement the next time we prescribed a similar set. As I write this section on Sunday, April 24, 2016, that day was yesterday's Saturday a.m. practice, during which we went some race-pace efforts for the main set with weight belts prior for a bit of a PAP effect. Athlete B was riding much higher in the water, and after I sought feedback she said that, yes, she was thinking about engaging the core and keeping her hips high. It was not that she couldn't complete the previous set in which she had the lower hips—she was simply not mentally engaged to do so.

A side note: This leads to a lesson for all coaches and athletes alike; it is one that we already know and perhaps need to be reminded of every now and then. Oftentimes it is not that a set is too hard, that the interval is too fast, or that the weight is too heavy and so forth. No, oftentimes a simple readjustment and refocus is all that is needed to excel in a given task . . . in sport and in life!

Increased General Muscular Strength, Power, & Endurance

Without getting specific, one could simply say that weight belts increase total body strength, power, and endurance. I did believe it appropriate to separate the core into its own category, however, as perhaps more so than any other swim training device, weight belts are specific to training the span of our bridge.

The extremities are not forgotten, however, and are also impacted in a positive way by weight-belt training, with the hands and feet again acting as the piers that must support the span. As Colwin previously stated, the weight belt forces the athletes to find the strongest leverage on the water—in other words, the strongest possible combination of lift and drag propulsion that maintains or improves body position and forward velocity. In short, they must work smarter and harder, much harder, with a heavy weight belt to maintain their speed and body position. Every up and down beat of the kick must be utilized to the fullest extent; every stroke taken must be at maximum velocity and moving from north to south in the classic straight-line pull. The heavy weight belts force the athletes to add efficiency to their maximal efforts, a rare concept that is hard to explain to them in words and often must be elicited naturally with a heavy Power Tower or weight-belt effort.

And similar to the heavy Power Tower efforts, we see similar benefits with heavy weight belts, namely an increase in muscle-fiber and motor-unit recruitment in both the arms and the legs. With regards to the legs specifically, it is amazing how a heavy weight belt can turn a "lazy" two to four-beat kicker into a solid six to eight-beat kicker in just a few sessions; the lazy kicker's legs simply sink unless she drives them with a tremendous effort while wearing a heavy belt.

In short, weight belt efforts will increase swimming-specific strength, power, and endurance, and while perhaps not specific enough for the principle of specificity devotees, I believe with certainty that there is a definite carryover to free, untethered swimming.

Specific Post-Activation Potentiation

The twenty-five-pound belt certainly elicits a much different response than our ten-pound belts at Penn State and earlier in program history here

Jake Shellenberger

at Liberty, and what a difference those fifteen pounds can make. I was not impressed with the PAP response of the lighter belts, as I noted, but the response from the twenty-five-pound belt is impressive, to say the least. In fact, the PAP response from the twenty-five-pound weight belt throughout the various sets we prescribe is on par with the response from heavy Power Towers, and in some sets the effects are even greater.

I cannot prove the following, but my hypothesis as to why the twenty-five-pound weight belt shows a greater PAP response in some cases than a heavy Power Tower is twofold:

Firstly, I believe the twenty-five-pound belt elicits a fight or flight response from the sympathetic nervous system, with adrenaline and noradrenaline rushing through the bloodstream before and during the effort and then staying elevated for the subsequent non-weight-belt effort that would follow. A Power Tower simply cannot recreate this response.

As to why I believe this, in short, there is a definite "fear factor" with using the heavy weight belts, specifically over deep water, and this is quite evident during dive max efforts at our pool here at Liberty, as we start in twelve feet of water with the pool gradually sloping up to four and a half feet at the turn end. I rarely see greater efforts than when our women dive max with a twenty-five-pound belt. At that point, at the core, cellular level, the survival instincts kick in, as our athletes know they have to go beyond maximum effort to get to the shallow end, where they can stand. I believe this is a healthy dose of fear, and we are careful to make sure we have spotters in place for such efforts, and the women know they can always unhook the weight belt if need be.

While the effects diminish over time as the women become more experienced with the heavy belt, imagine strapping on twenty-five pounds for the first time and diving into twelve feet of water—you are going to swim faster than you ever have before, and the PAP response will be quite evident on the next effort with no belt. Swimming coaches have always joked that they would see true maximum efforts if they could train with sharks in the pool—while obviously not nearly that extreme, the heavy weight belt in deep water does elicit a fight or flight response from the nervous system and in turn a greater PAP response, in some cases, than a heavy Power Tower alone.

Jake Shellenberger

Secondly, I believe the twenty-five-pound belt can engage more muscle groups and can recruit more motor units and fibers in said groups, causing a greater PAP response than a heavy Power Tower. While heavy Tower efforts engage the muscles of the shoulders, arms, chest, legs, and back, the weight belt adds the core in large quantities to the aforementioned groups, making for a true total-body PAP response. As an added benefit, the weight belt can also be used off the block for starts and for turns, making it a bit more versatile than the Tower.

And again, while the twenty-five-pound belt is exceptional for eliciting a PAP response, twenty-five pounds is only the beginning of what is possible, and we have women who are ready for the thirty and thirty-five-pound weights. I imagine we will see an even greater neuromuscular response from the heavier belts, and when the time is right (assuming I am "allowed"), I will look into making the purchase.

A few of my favorite weight-belt PAP sets and progressions for kicking, swimming, starts, and turns (assume several rounds of the following or a mixture of various sets . . . again the creativity is limitless):

3 X 12.5 Max Blast Swim with heavy weight belt, assorted gear or no gear at all
1 X 15 Max Blast Swim no weight belt

3 X 12.5 Max Blast Kick with heavy weight belt
1 X 12.5 - 15 Max Blast Kick no weight belt

3 X 15 Dive Max with weight belt, flat or relay, no fins
1 X 15 Dive Max, no weight belt, flat or relay, no fins

3 X 15 Yard turn sprints with medium to heavy weight belt (from just outside the flags to just outside the flags, allowing for proper approach to the wall and race specific dolphins and breakout after the turn)
1 X 15 Yard turn sprint, no weight belt

3 X 12.5 Max Blast Swim with heavy Power Tower with choice of gear if any

2 X 12.5 Max Blast Swim with heavy weight belt with choice of gear if any

1 X 15 Push Max with no toys with choice of gear if any

3 X 12.5 Max Blast Swim with heavy Power Tower with choice of gear if any

2 X 15 Dive Max with weight belt, flat or relay

1 X 15 Dive Max no weight belt, same flat or relay

2 X 20 Running Dive Max Swim with heavy weight belt

1 X 25 Running Dive Max Swim no weight belt for time to a hand or foot touch*

* This set is a lot of fun during our Florida training trip and during the summer here in Lynchburg. In both instances, we swim at outdoor pools with a concrete deck, allowing us the freedom to explore some of the limits I mentioned at the end of the previous chapter on Post-Activation Potentiation. This set has produced several nine-second 25-yard swims without a belt to a hand touch, and the women receive a PAP effect from the weight belt swim, *and* the run. Take the belt off, and watch them fly on the running dive!

3 X Weighted pull-up, from whistle start

2 X 15 Dive Max flat start with weight belt

1 X 15 Dive Max flat start with no weight belt

A few of many dream PAP sets I have and will implement when we have our concrete deck (assume generous rest intervals throughout):

3 X Heavy hang clean (or other Olympic lift)

2 X 12.5 Max Blast Swim heavy Power Tower with choice of gear if any

1 X 12.5 Max Blast Swim heavy weight belt with choice of gear if any

1 X 15 Max Blast Swim push or dive with choice of gear if any

3 X Heavy hang clean with weight belt on

2 X 15 Dive Max flat or relay with weight belt

1 X 15 Dive Max flat or relay no weight belt

3 X Heavy hang clean with weight belt on

2 X 15 Running dive max with weight belt

1 X 15 Dive Max flat or relay

3 X Weighted box jump with weight belt, stationary for flat start, relay step approach for relay starts

2 X 12.5 Dive Max flat or relay (same as box jump) with weight belt

1 X 15 Dive Max flat or relay (same as above)

2 X 20 Max Blast heavy Prowler push sled sprints with plates, weight belt on the athlete

1 X 15 Dive Max flat or relay with weight belt

1 X 15 Dive max flat or relay no weight belt

And many more!

Improved Technique & Force Application

As with the Power Tower, nearly any drill can be enhanced and any inefficiencies in the stroke magnified with a weight belt. As with drilling on the Towers, a light load should be used, relative of course, to the athlete's strength and experience level. We start our drilling progressions with the weight belts at five pounds, and we have women who are now drilling with as much as a ten-pound belt. It is amazing to see the progression—what we used at Penn State for training with our sprint women, we are now using for drilling here at Liberty. As Colwin led on, simply swimming by itself with a weight belt can be considered a drill, as the athletes will instinctively work technique by anchoring on hard, deep water with their hands.

Two of my favorite weight-belt drills:

1. The previously described "Arizona Drill"

This is the left paddle, right fin combo, and, again, this drill is fantastic for connecting the extremities diagonally through the core, and what better way to enhance this drill and magnify any inefficiencies than by . . . loading the core.

4 X 50 Left paddle, right fin, snorkel, with weight belt

4 X 50 Right paddle, left fin, snorkel, with weight belt

4 X 50 Both fins and paddles, snorkel, with weight belt

BONUS: 1 X 50 @ 93%, fins and paddles, no weight belt—you will see some incredible times here for fast but not max swimming!

We have several women who can easily handle heavier belts on this drill; the stronger and more skilled athletes can generate quite a bit of force through their cores and direct it through the right fin, left paddle combination.

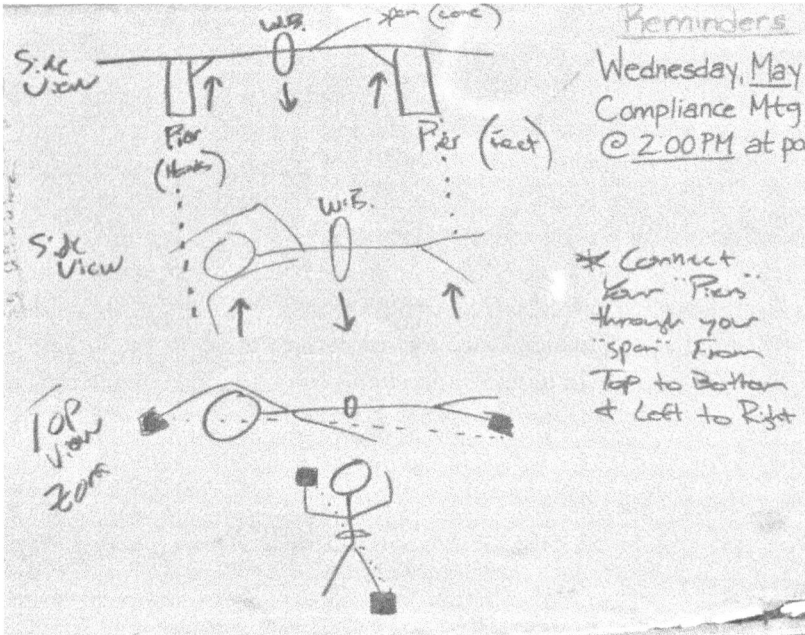

My attempt at explaining the Zona weight belts on our white board at practice. Thankfully the "art" of coaching is more intuition, soft skills, and theory than a literal interpretation!

2. Sculling and any subsequent variations

Imagine, again, the resisted core bridge in the weight room—have you ever desired your athletes to better transfer this position to the water, or, better yet, actually have them train this position with resistance in the pool? Sculling with a weight belt is your answer, and we scull quite a bit with weight belts here at LU.

The trick is to put the buoy (or two) at the ankles, as far away from the athlete's center of gravity and the weight belt as possible, without losing the buoy. The bridge is now complete, with the weight belt providing resistance over the span and the buoy and the hands acting as the piers, supporting the weight belt through the core. We receive quite a bit of positive feedback from our women with this drill, as they love the challenge of keeping their hips high and only using the core and a sculling

Jake Shellenberger

motion to maintain body position. Breaststroke and IM types will especially find this drill attractive, for they can switch between traditional sculling and a half breast scull or slight breast pull, at will.

Back to the debate on lift versus drag propulsion . . . Does a lift force aid in propulsion? Try this drill and see what your eyes and intuition tell you. Now, again, I do believe that drag propulsion is the primary mover, and we teach the aforementioned straight-line application of force across all four strokes, here at Liberty. As we know, however, a straight line is often not possible throughout the entirety of an individual stroke, and to say that lift does not contribute whatsoever to propulsion is quite short-sighted, in my humble opinion.

There are countless variations of this drill made possible when the buoy is moved to the ankles, and, again, nearly any drill can be modified in this way to produce the weighted core bridge with a stationary pier (buoy) and the propulsion pier (hands/forearm/upper arm, etc.).

A few of my favorites:

- Fly Pause
- Left/Right Arm Pulling
- Arizona 50s pulling or sculling, modified with no fins
- Example:
    o 4 X 50 With left paddle only
    o 4 X 50 With right paddle only
    o 4 X 50 Both paddles
- Anything with the Anti-Paddle

Anti-Paddle weight-belt drilling is quite advanced; it takes a highly skilled athlete with incredible core strength, the ability to hold water on the forearm, and an intense amount of laser-sharp focus to complete successfully.

My favorite Anti-Paddle weight-belt drill is pure vanilla (not much else is needed when already challenging the athlete in such a way) and should easily separate those with highly developed EVFs and swimming-specific core strength from all others:

"N" X 25 or 50, Pull Strong, with Anti-Paddles, buoy in ankles, snorkel, and a light to medium weight belt depending on skill level

If this drill doesn't teach the athletes to engage their forearms in the stroke . . . I don't think anything will! Again, this drill is advanced, and I would start with five pounds and go from there, if you decide to give it a try. Your athletes will love the challenge, and I believe they will learn much about propulsion in the process, whether consciously or subconsciously. If nothing else, they will be engaged mentally and highly focused—a drill set such as this one allows for no other options.

Weight-Belt Season Planning, Recovery, & Taper Considerations

As with the Power Towers, we follow a varied load and volume progression throughout each week and season here at Liberty, and we taper the weight belts in a similar fashion to the Towers. Refer back to the Pure Power taper considerations and season planning for more details. In short, September and early October feature lighter belts and more emphasis on technical work, while from October to the end of January heavy belts and Pure Power are a staple in our yearly plan.

Again, we use weight belts three to four times per week, with two heavy sessions focused on Pure Power and two lighter sessions focused on Power Endurance, drilling, pulling, and so on. There may be certain points in the year when we use weight belts more than four times per week, but any use above four times would not be a main set focus and, instead, would work drilling, pre-set usage, or Power Endurance.

A typical week in late October, for example, might see two heavy power sessions combined with one drill-focused session and a race-pace* session featuring Power Endurance work. We might also go two Power Endurance sessions combined with two heavy Pure Power sessions or any combination thereof, not exceeding two practices focused on heavy belts. I should note that these Pure Power and Power Endurance sessions on weight belts are often combined with Power Towers. Our sprint group will go three power-focused workouts per week, and it is within those three workouts when we will go two heavy power sessions, whether on Towers, just weight belts, or a combination of the two.

*An example of a race-pace main set with weight belts:

Three Rounds:

50 With Anti-Paddles—set the stroke!

12 X 25 @ :30 Max with a light weight belt, no gear

Extra: 30 take weight belt off

4 X 50 @ :60 Hitting 200 Goal Pace, free and back types to a foot touch

100 EZ

We went a similar set this spring, and it was quite challenging—the 12 X 25s with the light weight belt challenge and fatigue the athletes tremendously, and the four 50s at the end are a challenge to hit 200 goal pace.

Planned recovery workouts from the coaching staff and an emphasis on recovery outside of the pool are a must when using heavy belts. As with heavy Power Tower work, there is certainly a neuromuscular fatigue and training cost that must be considered when planning a week, and in turn, a season. Soft-tissue work in the weight room is of the highest importantance, and I would expect this to already be an emphasis in most college-level strength and conditioning programs. For club and high-school coaches, a few foam rollers would be a great introduction to the world of soft-tissue recovery for your athletes and can be purchased for minimal cost; many club and high-school programs already implement soft-tissue work in their routines and certainly do not need any advice from me on the subject!

Final Thoughts

In closing, to echo Sam Freas, "Weight belts are still very important. They flat out work, as do resistance and accelerated swimming" (Freas 2015, 94).

Admittedly, I was skeptical at first, and during my days at Penn State I rarely prescribed weight belts for our sprint types. I can now say with certainty, however, that yes, weight belts do work, and there is a ceiling for their usage that is much higher than previously thought by the coaching community. After seeing firsthand the benefits of the heavy belts and the PAP effects our women experience, weight-belt work is now a staple in our program, and combined with the Power Tower, forms the core of our power training for both sprint and distance types.

In regards to said ceiling, twenty-five pounds is well below the limit, and I am excited to see what the future holds as more coaches and athletes continue to experiment and to push the boundaries of what is thought possible.

Parachutes

We love parachutes here at Liberty, for three reasons specifically. First and foremost, parachutes are fantastic for their mobility; each one of our student-athletes has her own parachute and keeps it on her at all times in her equipment bag. Whether it be away meets, our yearly Florida training trip, swimming at home over Thanksgiving or Christmas break, our conference meet, or one of those rare occasions when a student-athlete chooses not to train with us in the summer, the parachute provides each of them with portable resistance on the go.

Secondly, parachutes are inexpensive and great for resistance on a tight budget. It is quite the investment to provide enough Power Towers for each team member to have her own bucket for a power-focused workout, but a chute for each is attainable for most, if not for the overwhelming majority of programs.

Lastly, the parachute provides a unique form of resistance in that said resistance is varied, dependent upon the speed at which the athlete is swimming. Similar to a body moving through water and frontal drag increasing as velocity increases, the chute will become "harder" as the swimmer increases velocity, and the athlete will need to generate more power or swim more efficiently to overcome the added resistance. Compare the chute to a Power Tower, which features a mostly uniform resistance from wall to wall, and one can see how this unique characteristic could be beneficial. I say *could be*, as although I want the change in resistance at times, this is highly coach dependent; not all coaches will feel the same about resistance changing throughout the swim.

Another unique aspect of the chute, which I cannot determine to be a positive or a negative, is the fact that not only does the resistance of the chute change as the athlete increases velocity, the actual position of the chute will change depending on the flow pattern of the water moving past and then behind the athlete. We instruct our women to place the chute belt and subsequent cord directly in the middle of the back, however the actual chute will "blow in the wind," so to speak, and never follow a straight-line path of resistance, as does the stationary Power Tower cord. Put another way, if the Power Tower cord does move, it was the body position of the athlete that changed, not the Tower. With a parachute, not only is the body going to change position naturally, body position could also be affected by the chute moving.

Some general thoughts here:

1. The "all-in" principle of specificity types would no doubt resist the parachute as per the body position argument.
2. Those in the middle of the debate have many questions.
3. Those who are more general in nature will have few objections to using the chutes.

As I fall in line with the third camp, we use chutes here at Liberty for the previously mentioned benefits, however I do have questions as to how much chute movement is acceptable in regards to the subsequent changes in body position produced by said movement. In short, the parachute will move during the swim, making it harder to achieve a straight-line pull and more efficient body position. The athletes will have to work harder, smarter, or a combination of both to adjust to, and to correct, these challenges. Is going through this process a net gain or loss?

I do not know the answer to this question, and it reminds me a bit of the negatives and positives of training in a pool with wave turbulence versus no turbulence. Is having to fight off a bit of wave drag and the changes in body position said drag causes a good thing? Certainly, too much turbulence has a detrimental effect on body position and, in turn, training—but do we want to eliminate wave drag altogether? If you take the principle of specificity to the extreme, with the goal of winning Olympic gold, we should all train long-course meters, year round, with one person per lane, and wear racing suits in the process, for we know that not wearing a suit will change body position for the worse. But of course we wouldn't train that way even if we could, because no one takes the principle of specificity to that extreme.

It is interesting, again, to note that there are coaches who would advise against parachutes (and weight belts, Power Towers, etc.) because of the adverse changes in body position these devices may cause. Yet, these same coaches are training multiple athletes to a lane, with plenty of wave drag created in the process, while not wearing racing suits, etc. Is a change in body position the real reason for not training with resistance? Do we as a coaching body (myself included) tend to pick and choose when we want to follow certain principles based on our previously determined biases, or are we making decisions using our full arsenal of science, logic, and reason? I will let you determine the answer.

VASA Trainer

The VASA Trainer is a great tool for developing upper-body swimming-specific strength and power on land, and we used this product quite often at Penn State, even taking four of them to Florida each year for our training trip. Ear infection? No problem. With the VASA Trainer you can still get a great upper body workout even if you cannot swim, and for that reason alone, they are a great investment for any program.

I think of the VASA as similar to a horizontal pull-up, with the goal being to increase the angle at which one uses the machine while still maintaining the classic EVF and high-elbow position. Imagine the strength needed to use a VASA trainer in this way at a ninety-degree angle to the pool deck. While probably impossible, I wonder how close we could get, and I plan to find out when we build our new facility. Deck space is at a premium right now, with eight Power Towers in a six-lane, 25-yard pool, but when we build our new facility we will invest in a few VASA Trainers and start to explore the limits.

Zona Pulling With Tubes

Arizona introduced me to a unique way of pulling, in which their distance crew primarily would pull with small riding-mower-type tire tubes around their ankles. The tubes were small enough to stay securely on the ankles even at high speeds, but large enough to provide a bit of drag when moving through the water and to keep the feet high. The drag is beneficial for obvious reasons, as it helps build swimming-specific strength and power, and by keeping the feet extremely high on the water, higher than normal, the athletes were forced to keep their cores engaged and keep their hips high.

We currently do not have any of these tubes here at Liberty, but I plan on investing in them and using them for weight-belt pulling, sculling, and other drills, and I foresee this being quite beneficial, as oftentimes the weight belts are heavy enough to sink the ankles with a normal buoy.

Looking back, I realize the tubes on the ankles for pulling is not unique to Arizona specifically; as this was the first time I was introduced to them, we use the term Zona Pulling in honor of their program.

Ankle Weights

I was introduced to ankle weights at Penn State, and we use them here at Liberty. Ankle weights are great for, again, developing swimming-specific strength and power, and not just in the legs. The core is also brought into play, as is the upper body; you simply must pull with more strength and power to overcome the drag caused by the ankle weights.

Ankle weights are fantastic for for PAP work; refer back to the PAP section for more on ankle weights and the greatest display of PAP I've ever seen with Ed Felty and our Penn State sprint crew. I have never seen a kick more powerful and explosive from the "baseline," if you will, and his legs found a whole new level of maximum effort after several PAP Power Tower efforts with ankle weights.

Weight Vest

We originally bought weight vests for our weight room workouts, specifically weighted box jumps and resisted pull-ups. Four years ago when our then strength and conditioning coach switched to dumbbells in the ankles for resisted pull-ups, we had the idea to bring the weight vests to the pool and experiment with weight vest swimming. For the benefits of weight vest swimming, refer to the section on weight belts. The two are interchangeable in many ways, with the weight vest simply changing the load point of the span from the hips to the upper body, or the hand "pier" of the bridge, if you will.

We use the vests sparingly; the weight belts are more versatile (we cannot dive with vests, for example), and thus we use the belts much more often.

Stretch Cords

The cords are what we thought they were, and I spoke at length about their usage for PAP work and for resistance training in the previous chapter. We use them primarily for meet-specific PAP work and for speed-assisted training in workouts. We do not use them much for resistance in training, as we have the Power Towers, parachutes, and weight belts; the above three are much more efficient and easier to use.

Two tricks with cords that we do use quite often:

Resisted Starts:

I was introduced to resisted starts with cords by Rick DeMont at Arizona and immediately implemented them into our sprint training at Penn State and then here at Liberty. This is a tricky technique for the coach to master, but, when mastered, it provides a safe and efficient resisted start for the athletes, helping to improve starting-specific strength and power, while also eliciting a PAP response from the upper and lower body.

The Technique:

1. Athlete wears cord belt around the waist, with the cord centered in the middle of the back. This is important, as you do not want the resistance of the cord to interfere with her balance on the start and when driving off the block.

2. Coach pulls the cord back to desired resistance, making sure to keep the cord high; ideally you want the resistance vector of the cord to match the athlete's entry angle into the water.

3. On start, athlete explodes into the water and coach lets out the slack in the cord.

Advanced Technique:

Loop the cord a second time through the belt for a double cord, or triple for your strongest athletes. For an even more advanced technique, add heavy weight belts to resisted cord starts, and challenge the athlete to explode through the cord and belt. A progression might look similar to:

Several Rounds:

1 X Weighted pull-up with a weight belt from a whistle start

1 X Resisted start with cord and weight belt

1 X 15 Dive Max for time with no weight belt or cord

See the photos on the following two pages for a progression of resisted starts. Be sure to have some slack ready in the cord to let out off the start; ideally we are resisting the start only, not the entry into the water. That is to say, there should be resistance up until the feet leave the block completely. Then, ideally, there is no resistance whatsoever when the hands hit the water. This requires quick action on the part of the coach—you must let out the slack quickly!

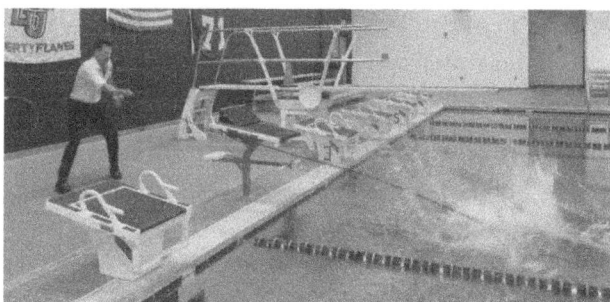

If you are new to resisted starts, begin with a single cord and your weakest athlete. My first attempt at a resisted start was at Arizona, on a double cord, with none other than Roland Schoeman on the blocks. Roland had the best start in the world, at the time, and he nearly pulled me into the water on my first try; it took every ounce of strength I had to stay dry!

Other Cord Drills:

25 Going 12.5 resisted, 12.5 LET GO and accelerate:

This is a neat drill that allows the athletes to go from resistance to no resistance immediately and to feel the subsequent acceleration to the wall. We use this drill quite often during taper, and our women love the feeling it provides.

The Technique:

1. Athlete starts with the cord belt around the waist, centered in the middle of the back.
2. Coach resists the swim to 12.5 mark—heavy!
3. At 12.5 mark coach releases the cord.
4. Athlete accelerates the final 12.5 into the wall with a race-specific finish.

Note: If you implement this drill, be sure to provide the resistance as close to the surface of the water as possible, as you do not want the angle of resistance to be too high. You also want to make sure you let go of the cord close to the surface of the water; you certainly do not want the cord to snap back and hit the athlete as she swims.

Another note, regarding the angle of resistance of cords in general: For all uses, said angle should again be low and as close to the water as possible. This goes for speed-assisted work with cords as well. I shake my head silently when I see coaches pulling athletes at meets at waist level or even higher; while I am not a fanatic about body position when it comes to resistance or speed-assisted work, if coaches can elicit better body positions in the water, why wouldn't they? By pulling the athletes at waist level or above, the body position does, in fact, change quite a bit, and the athletes look as though they are swimming uphill; this is not a position in which we want our athletes to swim, and especially ten to fifteen minutes before a finals race.

Here at Liberty, our coaching staff pulls our athletes as close to the water level as possible, with only the pool gutter system limiting us in this regard. We also teach our athletes to do the same when they pull each other, and I am confident that when performing sprint-assisted work, we are changing the body position as little as possible at high speeds. I have been tempted over the years to build a pulley system for cord pulling, specifically, that diverts the cord angle to horizontal, at the water surface. However, this would require drilling into the side of our pool to anchor the pulley. As is the case, I have decided to wait—perhaps we will look at building a similar contraption in the new facility.

Sprint-assisted work at Penn State circa 2008. Cords should be pulled as close to the deck as is possible for the coach or athlete to pull.

Jake Shellenberger

In closing, there are various ways one can train resistance for sprint and distance types alike, and while this book has focused primarily on Power Towers and their use, other forms of resistance do quite well in their own right and could be implemented alongside or in place of the Tower. As you can see, we use a variety of resistance toys here at Liberty, and, again, especially in the early season, I prefer the general base of strength and power that these various toys generate. The weight belts are of particular interest to me, as noted, and if we can say that Sam Freas made the weight belts popular, I will do my best to fully explore their limits.

While I do not yet know where the ceiling is, I know that twenty-five pounds is certainly not, and I am waiting patiently to train or to recruit the young woman with the strength, power, belief system, and attitude needed to find said limits.

Chapter 9: Tips, Tricks, & Innovations

"There's a way to do it better—find it."

Thomas Edison

I PLANNED for Chapter Nine to look at some of the opposition to re-sistance training, including literature cited by Dr. Brent Rushall, Dr. Ernest W. Maglischo, and more. I thought it fair to point out that not everyone believes in the power of the Tower and to provide a look into the belief systems and reasons as to why. As it turned out, I decided against a chapter on opposition literature, however I would encourage the reader to look into the studies referenced by the above two coaches and to ponder them deeply. It is never a bad idea to read, comprehend, and understand both sides of a discussion, and I believe wholeheartedly in the classical debate belief that one should be able to understand and argue the points of the opposition better than his or her own. If only we as a nation took the same viewpoint when it comes to politics! But I digress. The literature is out there, and I would point to Maglischo's epic work, *Swimming Fastest*, for his take and to Dr. Rushall's website for his.

Instead, I thought it more applicable to you, the reader, to share some of our power-training tips, tricks, secrets, and possible inventions/innovations that we've come up with over the years; as you are reading this book, you most likely already believe that resistance has a place in the training of elite athletes. I say *possible* because, to my knowledge, we are the first to implement these training concepts, but of course I cannot be sure. Perhaps there are coaches out there who have been doing this for some time—if that is the case, I have not seen it demonstrated publicly, and I apologize in advance for making the claim! As with the cord pull into a turn and resist, be sure to check out www.jakeshell.com for videos and supplemental information on the innovations described in this chapter.

Jake Shellenberger

Power Towers with Bands

We use strength training/power lifting bands over the shoulders in place of the stock belt around the waist for our Power Tower training here at Liberty, and two specific reasons I believe warrant this technique to be adopted by anyone using the Towers. This was an invention of one of our student-athletes, the aforementioned Meghan Babcock, who has a great mind for the sport and was a true student of swimming during her career here at Liberty. She was one who did not simply go through the motions in a workout and was always thinking about ways to be more creative and to improve our execution. I could always count on her to provide thoughtful feedback whenever we tried something new in practice, and I relied on her advice heavily throughout her four years in our program.

We originally bought the bands for dryland use, and Meghan had the brilliant idea one day to use them with the Power Tower over the shoulders in place of the belt on the waist. We use the orange Pro Light Resistance Band from elitefts, and you can find them on the web at elitefts.com if you want to try them out (and I highly suggest you do).

How To:

1. Remove the Power Tower belt, leaving the shock cord and open loop.
2. Place the band through the open loop, making sure to center the band in the loop.
3. Instruct the athletes to wear the band over each shoulder as they would a school backpack—this will work for fly, free, and breast.
4. For backstroke, simply cross the band in the front, and it will stay on the shoulders.
5. When placed properly on the shoulders, the band does not inhibit shoulder range of motion in any way—put on a backpack, for example, and one can still do windmills with the arms and so forth. The resistance from the Tower also helps keep the band on, and again, we do not have an issue with bands falling off during our Power Tower sessions.
6. Instruct the athletes to push off the wall centered, not on the side. While we normally push off the wall on our side, "leaving the wall

like an athlete" from a half-turn position, this will move the loop/band, and we want the resistance to remain centered in the middle of the shoulders/back.

7. I should note that centering the resistance is important in general—if using the included belt with the Power Tower, you always want the loop and shock cord centered squarely in the middle of the lower back.

Power Tower band setup:

Check out www.elitefts.com for a wide selection of bands and other strength and conditioning and dryland equipment.

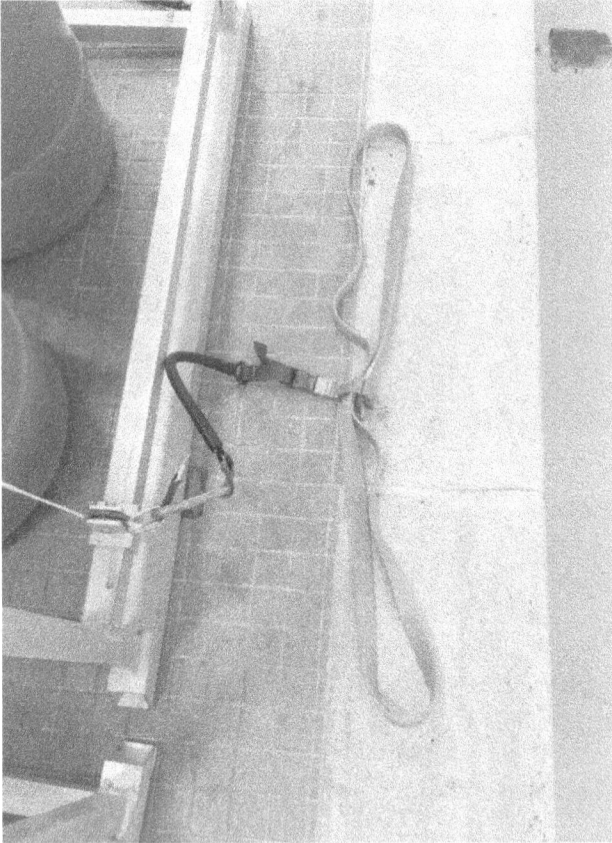

This setup also allows for much faster gear changes, as the athletes can "wear" the bands quickly and efficiently. For example, in a dive quality set we might go:

1 X 25 Dive Max, Rest five seconds at the wall, attach band

2 X 12.5 Max Blast Swim on the Power Tower, heavy bucket

Immediately take band off

50 Push Max

The standard Power Tower belt can become frayed, making quick changes much harder, and even when new, the belts are much slower to change than the bands.

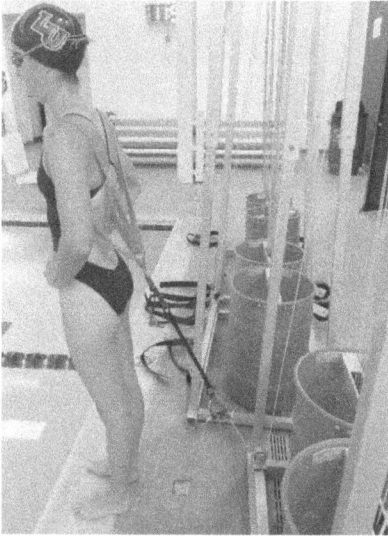

The athlete wears the band as though a school backpack. A main focus point: The band should be centered both in the loop that attaches to the Power Tower cord and on the shoulders. When using Power Towers with bands, we do not want our women pushing off the wall like athletes, as doing so will cause the band to become uneven on the shoulders.

Before pushing off, the athletes should get a bit of tension in the band and Power Tower cord to make sure the cord and band are centered. This may require moving the Towers away from the wall; as an added benefit to this technique, the push off the wall is also resisted with the full weight of the Power Tower bucket.

For backstroke, simply cross the band, and it will stay on the shoulder throughout the entire range of motion.

Jake Shellenberger

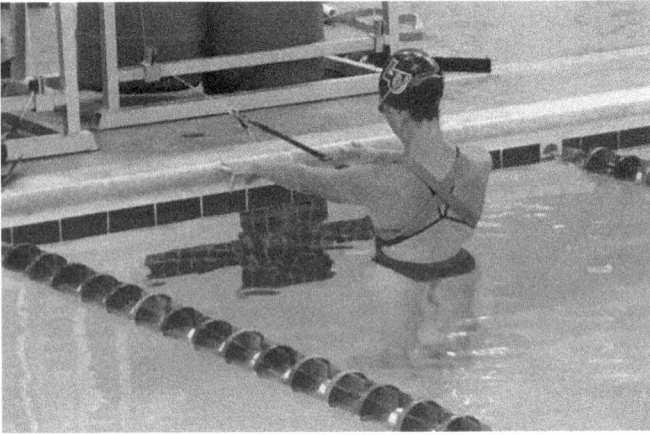

While the concept and setup are simple, the reasons are a bit more complex, but we believe it is the best way to use the Power Tower, and I would love to see more programs adopt this method of training. The bands are inexpensive, costing around $20 at the time of this writing, and are well worth the price for the following reasons.

First and foremost, the band changes the load point of the resistance of the Tower from the waist to the shoulders. Instead of feeling resistance from the hips down, the athlete feels resistance from the shoulders down, engaging the core in a way that belt simply cannot.

Imagine the weight room for a second—the Power Tower used with a belt around the waist is similar to squatting with the barbell somehow attached to your waist or squatting with a machine and a belt around the waist or hips. You completely miss the core engagement that comes from the barbell resting on the shoulders as in a conventional squat. The band placed around the shoulders on a Power Tower, then, more closely mimics a traditional squat in the weight room, and brings with it all the total body benefits that we see from said squats, namely core strength and engagement.

Our women love the feeling of said core engagement that must come when using the band on the shoulders, as you simply cannot have a loose or weak core when the resistance of a heavy Power Tower bucket is directed from your shoulders through your core, on through to the hips, and finally to the legs. You must engage the core with every stroke, and we believe this benefit does indeed transfer to free swimming without the Tower. The effects are more pronounced when bands are used with Power Towers for the Arizona Drill, in which you must connect the right paddle to left fin and so forth. With the band around the shoulders the core is "on fire" from top to bottom and left to right, and when performed correctly by elite athletes, a coach can clearly see the benefit of the bands in action.

Secondly, and perhaps more importantly, the bands around the shoulder are safer than the belt around the waist, specifically when using heavy buckets. I say *perhaps*, as the belt around the waist is not unsafe at lighter loads, and I do not mean to cause alarm where there is no immediate threat to athletes using Power Towers with light loads and the belt around the waist. This does change when you have strong athletes using heavy loads with larger paddles, for the following reasons:

We have several forces acting on the spine when using Power Towers, and to understand the following concepts better, I would advise the reader to brush up on compression and distraction as it relates to the spine specifically. While there is also torsion present, it is not significant enough to warrant our attention or discussion here. When using the belt around the waist, the spine is pulled away from the hands and backwards toward the Tower with a distraction force. The hands anchoring and pulling on water direct the body and subsequently direct the spine forward, causing the spine to be "pulled apart" at high speeds and heavy loads. Again, this is negligible at low weight but can be problematic with heavy loads and repeated use, specifically with athletes who are already hyper-mobile in the low back.

Distraction is not bad per se, and we prescribe distraction at times in the weight room as part of our soft-tissue recovery work. If anyone has ever used an inversion table or gravity boots, you know how good it feels to recover with distraction; I personally use both gravity boots and an inversion table after heavy deadlift sessions, as a way to counteract the extreme compression forces acting on the spine during my workouts.

This leads me to a second point: While distraction is beneficial in specific and controlled situations, the spine is much stronger when stressed via compression than when under a distraction force. For an example, we

Jake Shellenberger

need look no further than elite power lifting and strength training in general. Humans can squat and deadlift over a thousand pounds, but it is doubtful that any human's spinal connective tissue could withstand anywhere close to the same load when pulling the spine apart with a distraction force.

At this point, the physics and medical professionals reading will point out that the athlete will stop swimming well before the distraction force is able to actually pull apart the connective tissue, and yes, I would agree. But to use that logic to say that we should continue with distraction is to ignore the chronic stress and the cost of repeated distraction over time, regardless of whether that athlete is aware of it. This subtle tugging of the spine can lead to an increased risk of injury over the course of a season or a career. Compression is safer, and thus we use compression over distraction with our Power Tower training here at Liberty.

The feedback from our women has been overwhelmingly positive, as before the bands we did receive feedback of lower spinal soreness after heavy loads with the belt around the waist. The only negative feedback is that some of our breaststrokers report an adverse change in body position, as the bands do have a tendency to raise the upper body during the insweep of the stroke. If that is the case, we let them use the belt, as few breaststrokers can go heavy enough on the Towers to warrant the distraction force being a concern for an increased likelihood of injury. The one breaststroker in our program's history who did use heavy Towers (Emilie Kaufman, our school-record holder in the 100/200 and a 26.6 relay split) went with bands and reported no adverse body position; she was strong enough to use bands and a full bucket while swimming breaststroke without affecting her body position!

Power Towers with Bands and PVC Pipe Kicking

We bought PVC pipes for dryland use with the bands, using them for an ab circuit that would be much too complicated to explain here. The PVC pipe with bands and Power Towers was an invention of mine that took the concept of the Power Tower load through the shoulders and subsequently through the core to the next level—resistance "overhead" from the hands down to the feet. The catalyst was the weight room and the push press/jerk, specifically, with the progression in my mind looking something similar to:

1. If the Power Tower belt around the waist is similar to squatting with a barbell attached to the waist . . .
2. And the Power Tower with bands around the shoulder is similar to traditional squatting with the barbell on the shoulders . . .
3. Then somehow attaching the Power Tower bands to the hands would simulate an overhead barbell lift in the weight room.

Thus, the PVC pipe idea popped into my head, and we experimented with dolphin and flutter kicking on the Power Tower with the athletes holding the PVC pipes overhead, with the bands attached to the pipes and in turn the Tower. Again, the idea was to load the entire body, as we would in the weight room. Imagine if we could somehow kick flutter or dolphin in the weight room with a load overhead, needing to support the load through the arms, shoulders, core, legs, and feet. While obviously not possible in the weight room, it is certainly possible on Towers with bands and a PVC pipe in the pool. We don't use this drill often, but when we do, our women report an intense feeling of needing to "squeeze" the body from the hands to the feet. I have experimented with this myself, and, yes, you must absolutely fully engage the entire body to successfully complete this drill.

We almost always use fins with this set, but one would not necessarily need to do so. We do not use heavy buckets, as the intent is not pure strength or power but more so learning to fully engage the core from the hands to the feet, and in this case, we would define the core as everything from the wrists to the ankles. If we go back to the weight belt section and imagine a bridge, the piers would be the PVC pipe and hands on one end, with the feet acting as the pier on the other end. The span would be everything between those two points, loaded with a horizontal resistance.

As in the weight room, when working with a barbell, if attempting this drill, you must absolutely reiterate to the athletes the importance of balance and of making sure the pipe, bands, and Power Tower cord are all centered.

Again, imagine an overhead lift in the weight room with a barbell.

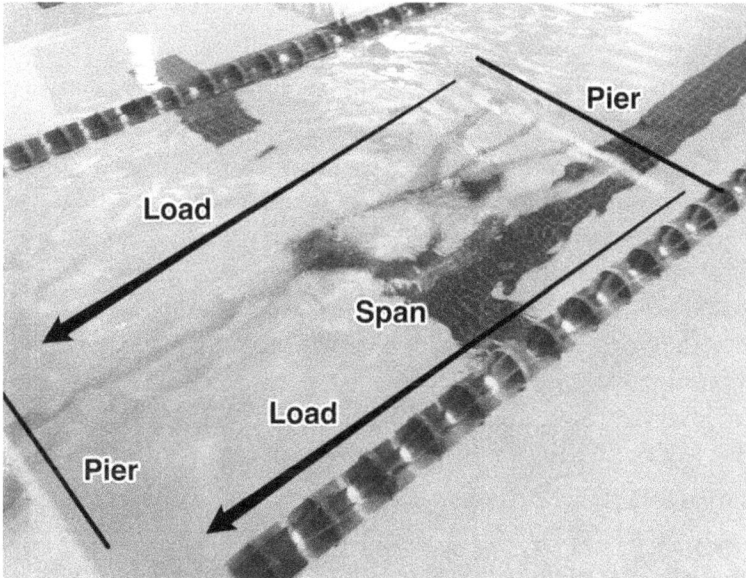

As an example set for the PVC kicking, we might go the following. Assume that all of the kicking is underwater body dolphin:

Three Rounds:

1 X 12.5 Max Blast Kick with Drag Sox

1 X 12.5 Max Blast Kick with Power Tower, band over the shoulders, light bucket, no fins

1 X 12.5 Max Blast Kick with Power Tower, Band on the PVC Pipe, light bucket, no fins

1 X 15 Max Blast Kick for time, no toys, no fins

While the bucket my not be heavy enough in this example to elicit a great PAP effect, the muscles of the core and shoulders are engage to the fullest, and this progression will produce fast efforts on the final 15 with no toys and no gear. If you want to give this a try, be sure to start with a light bucket!

PVC Power Scull With Weight Belt From Whistle Blast

I again took the weight belt bridge concept and expanded upon it, with a little inspiration from an old sprint training video David Marsh and Championship Productions created back in 2004, entitled "Swimming Faster the Auburn Way: Training and Race Strategies for Sprint Freestyle." In the video, David introduces the viewer to the concept of float sprinting with reaction training, and we use this training method extensively with our sprint types and our entire team here at Liberty. The concept is simple:

1. Athlete assumes a float position, with a flat body, head in line, arms outstretched.

2. On a whistle, athlete reacts and sprints a prescribed distance.

This sprint drill trains reaction time, power production, and rate-of-force development, as the athlete must learn to go from zero to sixty in as little time as possible. Again, I expanded upon the concept with weight belts and the PVC pipe:

1. Athlete wears fins, paddles, snorkel, and heavy weight belt.

2. Athlete starts in standing position.

3. On first whistle, athlete lifts feet up to rest on the PVC pipe, at the water surface, being held there by two partners, one on each side of the pipe.

4. Athlete engages in power sculling, burning out the forearms with a lift force while keeping the hips high by engaging the core.

5. After a certain amount of time, at the coach's discretion, the athlete reacts to a second whistle and sprints a prescribed distance, all-out max.

This drill is fantastic for training several components of fast swimming, among them a powerful sculling motion, the core, the legs, and maximum, all-out power sprinting in general. This is a challenge and is one of our sprint group's favorite power drills. We go up to the twenty-five-pound belts, here, and our strongest women can handle up to thirty seconds of power sculling with the heavy belt before the forearms start to fail. Depending on the weight of the belts we use, I will have them scull anywhere from five to fifteen seconds; we could scull longer, and perhaps I will try at some point, but a fifteen-second power scull followed by a seven-second all-out, max-effort swim is right where we want to be. This is a fantastic drill for breaststroke types, as the power sculling is right down their alley and takes incredible strength in the forearms to keep the hips high.

This drill can also be done without fins, and many times we will go sans fins for our breast types. If you try this set without fins, be sure to instruct the two athletes holding the PVC pipe to move it down and backwards as soon as possible after the whistle blast, as you do not want the person swimming to hit her feet on the pipe.

Power Tower Float Sprinting from a Whistle Reaction

This again borrows from Marsh's float sprinting concept but adds the Power Tower. This drill is challenging and is excellent for separating those who have power and those who think they have power. The concept matches the float sprinting described previously:

1. Athlete wears snorkel, fins, and paddles, with band on shoulders attached to Power Tower, with buoy in the ankles as to keep the feet from sinking during the float.

2. Athlete floats far enough away from the end of the pool for the Power Tower bucket to be off the ground, thus providing the initial starting resistance that must be overcome. The bucket cord is held in place by another athlete at the wall to prevent the Tower from pulling the athlete backwards, however we do want a bit of tension in the cord to provide the initial starting resistance.

3. On the whistle, the person holding the cords lets go as quickly as possible, and the athlete on the Tower blasts a prescribed distance against the resistance of the bucket.

Starting position: We are looking for a neutral spine, a neutral head position, and a relaxed scull/float motion with the hands. On the whistle . . .
MAX!

Another benefit to this drill is, of course, the training of reaction time—and not just reaction time, reaction combined with a maximum effort from the legs and arms. I am confident that this will carry over to our starting power off the blocks when we summon a max effort from the arms and legs following a horn/beep reaction.

This is a fun drill that our women love; again, this separates those who have a higher percentage of fast-twitch fibers from those who do not. A coach can easily see who can summon a high rate-of-force development, as, depending on the weight of the bucket, it takes an extremely high amount of power and said force development to get the bucket moving and to complete the swim. We will normally go 15s max here, which, when subtracting the distance away from the wall, is more in the 10 to 12-yard range.

Because of the extremely high power output and rate-of-force development produced, this set and the many variations one can prescribe is ideal for PAP work, and, as an added benefit, you are also training the reaction time of the athletes. I will list several example PAP-style sets featuring Power Tower float sprinting, with a few dreams I will attempt to implement when our new facility is built. Assume several rounds of each set if standalone or once through if part of a larger power circuit of multiple rounds:

3 X Weighted pull-up from a dead hang whistle blast

2 X 15 Max Blast Swim from a float with whistle reaction, with Tower, with heavy bucket, with choice gear

1 X 25 Dive max, flat start, no gear, to a foot touch for time

2 X Trap bar deadlift, heavy, from a whistle reaction

2 X 15 Max Blast Swim from a float with whistle reaction, with Tower, heavy bucket, with choice of gear

1 X 25 Max Blast Swim from a float, with whistle reaction, with choice of gear, no Tower, no breath

3 X Hang clean, heavy, from a whistle reaction, rest :30 between each effort and dropping the bar between efforts

2 X 15 Max Blast Swim from a float with whistle reaction, with Tower, heavy bucket, with choice of gear

1 X 50 Dive max, no gear, with touchpads in

3 X 15 Max Blast Swim from a float with whistle reaction, with Tower, heavy bucket, with choice of gear

Rest :60

2 X Weighted box jump, from a whistle start reaction

2 X Weighted pull-up from a dead hang with whistle start reaction

Rest :60, visualizing final heat of the 50 free at conference

1 X 25 Dive max, no gear, to a foot touch*

*If the above set doesn't stimulate maximum central nervous system readiness, I don't think anything will. Speaking of, PAP-style training with these types of loads is a great way to test for the overtraining of sprinters. This set should elicit much faster efforts than a regular dive 25 without the PAP stimuli, and the effect should be noticeable to the naked eye without a watch. If it does not, you may have some tired thoroughbreds!

Power Tower Float Sprinting from a Reverse Whistle Float

This is the ultimate in float sprinting drills that we prescribe here at Liberty, and I was hesitant to add this to the book, as this has been a closely guarded secret of ours over the last six years. This is insanely challenging, for lack of a better term, but a lot of fun for the pure sprint types and for those who enjoy power and strength training in general, whether in the pool or in the weight room. Few methods that we use elicit a greater force production and PAP effect than this drill, and I cannot begin to imagine the power required to move the bucket here against heavy loads. The concept is similar to the Power Tower float sprinting, although I will take credit for "inventing" the reverse float aspect:

1. Athlete wears snorkel, fins, paddles, with band on shoulders attached to Power Tower, with buoy in the ankles as to keep the feet from sinking during the float.

2. Athlete initiates the float further away from the end of the pool to allow for the reverse float and for the Power Tower bucket to be off the ground, thus providing the initial starting resistance.

3. The bucket cord is held in place by another athlete at the wall until the athlete is in floating position.

4. On the first whistle or hand drop, the athlete holding the cord begins to pull it backwards toward the wall, causing the athlete swimming to float backwards. At this point you can make the drill still more challenging by varying the speed in which the athlete at the wall pulls the cord backwards, and by the amount of water in the bucket. We start with a slow reverse float and a 1/3 bucket for freshmen, while at the top end we have athletes that can go a full bucket while floating backwards rather quickly—it must be seen to be believed!

5. On the second whistle, the athlete swimming blasts a prescribed distance, normally, again, out to the 15 but in the case of heavy buckets and fast floating, to the 12.5 mark.

Wow. This drill is impressive to say the least. A full bucket Power Tower is a challenge. A full bucket Power Tower from a dead float is harder still. A full bucket Power Tower effort from a reverse float, moving backwards at a decent speed is the "hardest" type of Power Tower training that we do here at Liberty. To reverse the direction of the Power Tower bucket takes an incredible amount of strength, power, and rate of force development, and when executed correctly by elite athletes, this is an absolute joy to watch.

Bonus: If this sprint drill isn't enough, try adding a weight belt to the mix for an even greater challenge. With the weight belt, you are now engaging the core on the reverse float, then engaging the core once more on the

Jake Shellenberger

second whistle during the blast swim. Only the strong need attempt this variation!

How To Properly Empty the Power Tower Buckets

This might seem trivial, but yes, there is a specific way to empty the Power Tower buckets if using water, that will lessen the number of headaches for you as a coach and will also increase the lifespan of your pulleys. Picture force vectors in physics and the direction of the force as it relates to the Power Tower cord and pulleys. Ideally, the force vector of the Power Tower cord, string, or whatever you want to call it "stays on the same vector," as it would when using the Tower. That is to say, when you empty the Tower you want to turn the bucket ninety degrees so that when tipped, the force vector of the cord hits the pulley squarely, as intended, not from the side, which can damage the pulley and cause the bearings to become loose and fall out. This is a simple fix that can save you a lot of frustration (and money) over time. If moving the Towers with weight or water in them, they should be moved the same way, with the bucket rotated ninety degrees to keep the force vector of the cord matching that of the pulleys.

One can see how the force would hit the pulleys sideways.

Ouch. Your pulleys will be hurting.

Force vectors aligning properly with the pulleys.

A bit silly? Perhaps . . . but when emptying heavy buckets, you absolutely want to use this technique!

Up until this chapter in the book, I haven't taken much credit for inventing the techniques and training methods described, for they are a blend of the many mentors I have had along the way (refer to the acknowledgements for a refresher). David Marsh's and Sam Freas' ideas also have an influence, combined of course with my own. But for the aforementioned concepts, specifically using the bands/PVC pipes on the Towers and the Power Tower reverse float sprinting, I would love for our program to be referenced for their "invention," if you will. Meghan Babcock devised the bands on the Towers, and I invented the reverse whistle float sprinting.

By all means, feel free to experiment and to use them in your program, but please, let your athletes and fellow coaches know whence these ideas came. I did not write this book to brag or to boast, but for the above two ideas, I would be untruthful if I told you I did not want Liberty and our program to have the credit for their invention. And can you fault me? What innovator wouldn't want his or her organization associated with a new device, technology, or training technique?

Chapter 10: Strength Training for Sprint Swimming

"It's always a good thing to get stronger. If you can get the women strong like the men, they're going to go fast. If you can get the men stronger, they'll be faster too."

Frank Busch

As I stated in the introduction, the original plan for the book included ten chapters, with no specific thoughts on strength training for sprint swimming, although I did plan on including general thoughts throughout. During the revision and editing process I realized that yes indeed, a chapter specifically dedicated to strength training for sprinting should be included, as a way to summarize and concentrate my thoughts and to add a bit more to the topic that was not covered in other parts of the book.

I have several strongly held beliefs regarding strength training for swimming and sprint swimming specifically, and I approach the subject from the unique angle of a strength training background combined with swim coaching. As mentioned in the introduction, I wrote and conducted our strength training and dryland sessions for our sprint group at Penn State, and was able to do so in large part because I was also a Certified Strength & Conditioning Specialist (CSCS) through the National Strength & Conditioning Association (NSCA).

Note: The strength coaches reading this are no doubt rolling their eyes at this point, and as such, let me speak to them directly to explain the situation in more detail. Yes, I agree with you, and I understand completely that a CSCS certification does no more to say one is a "strength coach" than a license does to say that a seventeen-year-old is an experienced and competent driver. Yes, I understand that a CSCS means little in the strength and conditioning world and that experience, the quality of mentors, and results trump certifications in the minds of the great strength coaches throughout the profession. I get it. My motivation for obtaining

the CSCS was simply to expand my knowledge of strength-training practices and to feed a passion that I had (and still do have) for "heavy . . .
weight." (The strength coaches in the crowd will get that reference.)

I also thought it another tool on the belt, if you will, a way to make myself
more marketable in the swim-coaching world and to help get a foot in the
proverbial door. Coming from a humble Division II background and being a poor-to-average swimmer myself, I needed all the help I could get.
Thus, after graduating from Shippensburg, I obtained the CSCS and did
what I could to market myself to DI head coaches. While having a CSCS
or other similar certifications doesn't make one a strength coach anymore
than an ASCA Level I certification makes one a swim coach, when you're
twenty-two and looking to break into the college coaching world, it certainly doesn't hurt either.

Back to strength training and my thoughts: In short, strength training is
of high importance for sprint types and of all strokes. Aside from technical excellence and the basic physiological benefits of training, I rank
strength and power at number three on the list of the trainable physical
attributes that lead to fast swimming (genetic factors such as height and
limb length not included). The details are a bit unclear, if you will, and are
up for debate, but the basic premise remains: strength and power are indeed important and play large roles in fast swimming. Regardless of what
some pockets of research tell us, I believe the above to be true, and I
believe it simply must be true for many reasons, chief among them being
the sheer fact that men are faster than women.

This is a topic I pose in question form quite often during the recruiting
process, when I mention the importance of our strength training and dryland programs here at Liberty, and to this date, some six years into our
program's history, not one recruit of hundreds has answered the question
incorrectly. It is amazing that every seventeen-year-old girl who is given
this question gets it right, while some in the coaching community with
many dignified titles and letters after their names still get it wrong. The
question is simply this, and I ask it to every student-athlete we recruit here
at Liberty: Why are men faster than women? It isn't a trick question, and,
again, the recruits get it right every time, without hesitation.

"Well, they're bigger and stronger."

Or some combination of the two, they say, and I immediately follow with a classic one-liner to the tune of:

"Yes! Absolutely. It certainly isn't because the boys work harder, that's for sure!"

Which without fail always elicits a laugh and an ear-to-ear grin from recruits and parents alike. Compare the team GPAs of high-school boys' and girls' swimming & diving programs for more, or take a look at the average GPAs of men's and women's college teams across an entire athletic department. More often than not, the women's team GPAs will be higher, for no other reason than the women simply work harder, all things considered, more often than not.

With that being said, as this is a book about power training for swimming and you are reading it, I am guessing you are in the camp that does believe that strength and its application to the water is important, and so I'll get back to it.

Let me first say that we are blessed here at Liberty to have a fantastic strength & conditioning department, and our head coach, who oversees the program, Bill Gillespie, is one of the best in the business. I have also been blessed personally to have a variety of strength coaches work with our swimming & diving program over the years, and I have had the opportunity to learn much from their time with our program. Each coach brought something different to our approach, and each one was more than willing to share the why of what he or she prescribed. Our department-wide strength-and-conditioning philosophy here at Liberty is the envy of many swimming coaches across the country. We train each sport according to its specific physiological characteristics and strength/power needs; there is not a one-size-fits-all approach here at LU, as there might be at other programs. One of the main grievances I hear from colleagues is that strength coaches tend to train everyone as though football players, and I am delighted that our department takes a different approach here at Liberty.

Our current strength coach, Shelton Stevens, is well rounded in his background, having worked with a variety of different sports over the years, and, while I hesitate to say that he has any one specialty, he has worked with baseball and volleyball specifically at nearly every school on his résumé. When I think of sprint swimming and the type of strength-and-conditioning approach I would prefer to see, a baseball and volleyball mindset, with a strong focus on the health of the shoulders, combined with explosive jumping ability and all-around athleticism . . . I don't think it gets much better! I spoke with Shelton before writing this chapter, and he has agreed to answer any specific questions about our program; feel free to contact him directly with any thoughts you might have. You can also read more on his blog at

http://shelton-stevens.wix.com/coach

or on Twitter: @SheltonGStevens.

Shelton is fantastic, for lack of a better term, and again, from his baseball/volleyball background, understands completely the shoulder and the demands of the repetitive overhead motions we see in baseball, volleyball, and swimming. There is a focus on strength, power, the health of the shoulder, and also the stability of the joint, and again, I cannot think of a better strength background from which to approach our sport. If you have the opportunity to work with a strength coach who is well-versed in baseball or volleyball, by all means, do it.

As an added benefit, my personal beliefs on strength and power for swimming mirror his perfectly, right down to exercise and equipment selection, programming, general physical preparation, taper, and so on and so forth. This is a huge boost and benefit to our program, and, again, it is a blessing to have someone in his position who "gets it" when it comes to swimming and who is on the same page as the coaching staff.

With regards to my personal beliefs, in the following sections I will share five general thoughts I've formed over the past ten years with regards to strength training for sprint swimming. As the goal of this book is in-water power, I will not get too detailed with the land aspect, but again, I did want to share, as I mention strength quite often throughout this work.

Jake Shellenberger

General Thoughts

"A rising tide lifts all boats."

While traditionally accredited to John F. Kennedy, the above quote originated much earlier, circa 1910, from Henry B.F. McFarland, and sums up my general thoughts in regards to strength training for sprint swimming perfectly. If we go back to the original example of why men are faster than women, the obvious and first reason that comes to mind is that men are bigger and stronger, and, again, our recruits nail it every time. There are of course other factors at play that we don't discuss with said recruits, including testosterone and estrogen levels, red blood cell count, heart and lung size, body composition, and the percentage of fast-twitch muscle fibers, among others. But to keep it simple, and in the general sense, men are faster because they are bigger and stronger, and Frank was spot-on with his analysis in the quote that opened this chapter. Watching the Arizona women lift was an experience; they embraced the weight room fully and ran the show, so to speak, outperforming the men by comparison, in both the sheer amount of weight lifted and in the intensity with which they attacked the sets and reps. Imagine a football team in the weight room during a heavy lift or a max day—that is the intensity the Zona women brought to the weight room nearly every day, often getting loud and yelling at each other in the process (always in a spirit of encouragement, of course).

And they were (and are) strong, incredibly strong, and not in any specific sense—more so with a general base of strength that they then transferred to the water. I hesitate to say they had a specific lift or muscle group that was "better" than another, for they were strong everywhere, whether it be Olympic lifts, legs, core, pull-ups, various other upper body lifts, etc.

And so I believe a rising tide lifts all boats. That is to say, while, yes, I agree with the principle of specificity in that we should eventually target the prime movers in our sport, my first general thought in regards to strength training for sprint swimming is that we should start with a wide base of general strength and then work toward specifics in the spirit of the principle of specificity.

Jake Shellenberger

It has been my experience over the years, and I have always believed (and I have no doubt the majority of coaches reading would agree) that all-around better land athletes, in the general sense, make the best sprinters, and this simple case in point provides solid evidence for the belief of a base of general strength. The old aphorism *you are only as strong as your weakest link* is another way to describe this phenomenon. Sam Freas was and is adamant on this point, and a look into his dryland/strength training programs from his two *Sprinting* books shows the wide base with which he also trains his sprinters.

Again, men are faster than women because they are stronger in the all-around general sense, not just because they are stronger in the lats, pecs, or other prime movers specific to swimming, and thus a wider, stronger base of general strength for both men and women is important for fast sprinting. As for how to acquire this base, I again agree with Freas here and have always believed that a gymnastics background should be "mandatory" for all young athletes, in any sport. That is to say, before starting football in grade school for example, I believe these young athletes should spend a few years in a beginning gymnastics program. The proprioception, general body awareness, flexibility, and emphasis on body weight exercises creates a solid general base of strength and skill that athletes can then use to better excel in their specific disciplines.

We have all heard the stereotype that swimmers are, in general, poor land athletes, and while I loathe to admit it, behind most stereotypes is a hint of truth—it is rare to find elite land athletes in the pool. Imagine if all swimmers, sprint and distance alike, started out in our hypothetical mandatory gymnastics program and then approached our sport from this general background. We would have better overall athletes, and no doubt swimming as a whole would benefit tremendously.

For the high-school or college athlete who missed this pivotal early childhood learning stage, all is not lost, and a good strength and conditioning coach or club/high school swimming coach can make large improvements in this base of general strength with a well-rounded and well-programmed strength training and dryland program. For the high school athletes, I side with the old-school, more traditional approach, and do not believe that high-school swimmers need to lift weights, specifically. I've always thought it foolish when I hear of high-school swimmers getting

Jake Shellenberger

into the weight room and putting plates on the bar without first being able to do a free-weight body squat with perfect technique, or to hold a core bridge with any degree of acceptable spinal alignment.

To say that a few high school/club swimmers (and college athletes too!) attempt to put the cart before the horse is an understatement to say the least. We have had such athletes here at Liberty, who, by no fault of their own, came into our program with previous weight-room experience but could not squat properly, hold the aforementioned core bridge, or complete a single strict-form pull-up. This is an issue that plagues many a college coach, and unfortunately I foresee this being a challenge for some time to come. In a perfect world, my ideal freshman sprinter would have progressed through the following in their grade and high school years:

1. Gymnastics first—early and often
2. Swimming and any other sports they want to play throughout grade and middle school (volleyball ideally!), while continuing a gymnastics-style, body-weight dryland program
3. Transition to full-time swimming in high school, building an aerobic base and competency in all four strokes; continuation and progression of the gymnastics-style, body-weight dryland program, with an introduction to proper strength training technique, focusing on traditional core and Olympic lifts using a wooden dowel rod or PVC pipe
4. Our hypothetical ideal sprinter would then enter our program as a freshman being able to do seven strict-form pull-ups, free-weight squat with perfect technique, perform the various Olympic lifts with ideal technique using a dowel rod, and have a wide base of general land athleticism and body-weight strength.

As for point three, while I do not believe high-school-aged athletes need to be strength training in the traditional sense, I would love to see them learn proper lifting technique with body weight or a dowel rod, and this is something that could even start earlier than their high school years. My fifteen-month-old son can squat with perfect form—what happens between then and eighteen years, when some athletes lose the ability? I see no issue with teaching proper squat, overhead, various Olympic, or other lifting techniques with a dowel throughout grade and middle school, as these are "life lifts" that are natural to the body, and these early years are the best time to learn.

Consider a hypothetical sixth grader, for example, who might have a school backpack that weighs twenty pounds or more. Our sixth grader approaches the backpack in the morning, ready to head off to school, and in one fluid (or sometimes not so fluid) motion, lifts the backpack off the ground with one arm and slings it over her shoulder. While the average parent sees just that, a backpack over the shoulder, I see a one arm kettle-bell power clean from the floor to the shoulder, and as such, I see no issue with teaching proper Olympic lifting techniques to grade schoolers and to high-school-age athletes using a wooden dowel. It certainly will make the transition to a college-level strength-and-conditioning program much easier!

To summarize general thought number one, a wide base of general strength and all-around athleticism are important for sprinters, and coaches should put a high priority on developing athletes in these areas before moving on to more specific strength work.

Testosterone Is Key

My second general thought regarding strength training deals with hormones, and unfortunately this is a sensitive subject for some. In reality, it shouldn't be—if coaches and athletes alike are serious about fast sprinting, especially for women, influencing hormone levels through strength training and *other legal means* should be of the highest priority. Testosterone is key, and the more of it that sprinters have, men or women, the faster they will be. Strength, power, body composition, the mental game and so on and so forth—the list of positives for higher levels of testosterone for men and women, and especially female sprinters, is exhaustive to say the least. Why are men faster than women? They have size and strength, as I noted, among other attributes, many of which can be simplified even further to one word: testosterone. Why are men stronger, for example, to break it down further? In my humble opinion, the single biggest factor is testosterone and the subsequent physiological changes it produces. It is not work ethic, desire, self-discipline, attention to detail, etc. No, the over-riding reason why men are stronger, and in turn faster, is simply that men have higher levels of testosterone.

Testosterone, as we know, plays a significant role in strength and power production and, in turn, fast sprinting. This simply must be true, if for no other reason than testosterone is a banned substance by WADA, and if it had no performance-enhancing effects for men and women it wouldn't be banned. *Naturally* increasing testosterone, then, should be a prime fo-cus for the strength-training and nutritional plan for a sprint swimmer. In reality, it should be a complete lifestyle plan. Strength training is only one piece of the pie, and the strength coach, sports nutritionist, athletic train-ing staff, and swimming staff should partner in an attempt to raise testosterone levels for sprint swimmers, especially women, as high as is possible for them to *naturally* do so.

What would a hypothetical plan include for a sprint swimmer? In a perfect world, I would love to see the following, for both men and women:

From the Strength Coach:

Heavy compound lifts as a staple in the strength-training plan, combined with "GH" (Growth Hormone) circuits that will elicit maximum levels of HGH secretion. I won't get into the science of how and why GH circuits work, but if you want more information, check out the article "GH Cir-cuits Reloaded" by Erick Minor as a great introduction to the science. Proper recovery and sleep should also be emphasized; as we know, tes-tosterone production requires sleep, and HGH is secreted when we sleep as well. Poor sleep quality or not enough sleep will not raise said testos-terone or HGH levels to optimal levels.

From the Sports Nutritionist:

The diet can and should be altered to favor testosterone production and to decrease estrogen levels. The science is varied here, thus I will not get into the details, but testosterone levels can absolutely be raised by adjust-ing the diet, and they should be. Consider also that increased body fat can lower testosterone levels and increase estrogen, making adherence to a proper diet all the more important. Alcohol lowers testosterone levels and increases estrogen, and as I mentioned previously, I believe we should do all we can to curb the binge-drinking culture found on the overwhelming majority of college campuses. As we all know, athletes are not immune to this culture, and in some cases are, in fact, major catalysts to the prevalence of said culture.

If I were coaching men again, the motivation to limit alcohol consumption would be easy—I would simply remind them that they are increasing their estrogen levels and lowering their testosterone levels with every drink, and the consequences for the extracurricular activities that they care deeply about are profound, indeed. We have seen that motivating college male swimmers by talking of heroics in sport and reaching their fullest genetic potential in the pool seldom breaks through . . . perhaps using other means to motivate men will have more of an impact.

Supplements, while somewhat taboo, can also be used to give the body what it needs to naturally increase testosterone levels. Among these, zinc and magnesium are key. Magnesium is a juggernaut, so to speak, and not only is it critical for testosterone production, it can and does aid in total-body and nervous-system recovery and stress reduction. Some seventy percent of the US population is believed to be magnesium deficient, and I would guess our student-athletes are no different. In a perfect world, all swimmers, especially sprinters, would supplement with zinc and magnesium, as I do not believe they are getting adequate amounts from their diets. Simply ask your athletes how often they consume dark-green, leafy vegetables, as one example.

Supplements are certainly controversial, and we can name on more than two hands the exhaustive list of scandals we've endured and athletes banned for their use. At the time of this writing, the Russian/Rio doping scandal is in full force, and unfortunately, supplements are oftentimes subconsciously lumped into the PED category. I am in favor of the use of NSF-certified supplements, and I believe they can in fact aid in performance and recovery in a safe way using natural ingredients.

There is much more in regards to diet—these are simply examples, and a sports nutritionist with knowledge of how the diet affects endocrine-system function will be able to point athletes to foods that have been shown in the literature to naturally raise free testosterone levels and to aid in recovery. By all means, don't take my word for it—the research is out there, and an expert sports nutritionist will be invaluable in this area.

Jake Shellenberger

From the Athletic Training Staff:

Sleep, recovery, sleep, recovery, and more of the same. See the points on sleep and the importance thereof with regards to testosterone production. Stress levels should also be monitored, and stress management techniques would ideally be prescribed from the athletic training staff. One of the surest paths to lower testosterone levels is poor sleep and a high-stress lifestyle. If this sounds as though describing the typical Division I athlete, oftentimes it is certainly quite accurate. Sleep and stress management are critical, and this is an area where I believe we can see large improvements from our athletes if we could somehow break through to them and nudge them to turn their phones off earlier, to sleep a bit more, and to stress a bit less.

At the absolute least, coaches and athletic trainers should instruct any athletes using iOS to use the Night Shift feature to block blue light coming from mobile screens at night; blue light suppresses melatonin secretion and leads to poor sleep quality. I have my Night Shift set to run automatically from 6 p.m. to 5 a.m., and am thus limiting blue light for some four hours before my 10 p.m. bedtime. If you are unfamiliar with blue light and its harmful effects on sleep quality, Google "blue light has a dark side Harvard Health Publications," and check out the great introductory article from Harvard Med.

Another area I would love to see athletic trainers address is that of xenoestrogens, or synthetic chemicals that mimic estrogen in the body, and that I believe absolutely do raise estrogen levels (which there is good evidence in the literature to support). This includes plastics, pesticides, skincare products, household cleaners, etc., and the list goes on and on. To date, I haven't seen many, if any, coaches or sport scientists address this issue, and I would love to see it become more mainstream in sport science and in coaching circles. By now, we have all heard of BPA-free water bottles, which are great, but the same athletes who buy the BPA-free bottles are still using the suntan lotion filled with benzophenone, plastic food storage containers, and skin-care products containing parabens and so forth.

My friends are always shocked to learn I haven't used sunscreen in many years, and we do not use plastic for food storage in our house—glassware

203

only. We also filter our shower water in the Shellenberger household and buy organic food whenever and wherever possible. We use organic laundry detergent that is xenoestrogen-free, and the same goes for soap and toothpaste as well—all organic and all free of the chemicals that raise estrogen levels in the body.

Of note: Male testosterone levels have been steadily declining since the 1970s as our use of these various products has increased. This fact, combined with our poor diets and inactivity, has caused our waistlines to expand to unprecedented levels. We love to tout ourselves as the greatest nation on earth, and while I am not here to debate such matters, it is a sheer fact that Mexico only recently overtook us as the heaviest nation on earth. This is a vicious cycle, as again, increased body fat in turn raises estrogen levels, and increased estrogen levels raise body fat. I am doing my part to combat this epidemic for myself and for my family—my hope is that more will join the cause, sprinters in the swimming world included.

Of note, reality: It would be foolish for coaches to think that collegiate sprint swimmers are going to give up their skin-care products in search of faster 50 freestyle times, but perhaps the athletic trainer, strength coach, sports nutritionist, and swim staff could do their part to move the athletes toward organic brands that limit or altogether remove the use of these xenoestrogens. It is possible, and our assistant coach here at Liberty, Jessica Barnes, and my wife, Lorin, are perfect examples. Their skin-care products are organic and chemical free, and while yes, they are more expensive, the fact that there are those out there who do value such things gives me hope that perhaps our athletes will do likewise.

From the Swim Staff:

Model the aforementioned lifestyle habits and practice what you preach. Use the resources on campus, and refer athletes through the proper protocols to those who can aid in improving lifestyle choices. Raising free testosterone is possible, and our sprint athletes have everything to gain and nothing to lose (except tenths off their 50 times) by doing so.

Free Weights > Machines

Jake Shellenberger

"We don't use machines, they don't allow the athletes to stabilize and generally aren't good for them."

Neil Willey
Arizona Strength Coach May 24, 2007

While this concept is now mainstream, it wasn't always this way, and thankfully nearly all strength coaches have made the switch. Much of the reason why I ended up coaching the PSU sprinters in the weight room dealt with machines, and I will leave it at that for you to fill in the gaps.

I am not sure there is much more I can add here that we do not already know or currently practice, but if coaches out there are struggling with a strength staff that does use machines for athletes, perhaps the above quote from Neil can help. I can guarantee he has coached more NCAA champions, Olympic gold medalists, and world-record holders than your strength coach who uses machines, and he is not the only elite-level-swimming strength-and-conditioning coach to make such a claim. Machines are inferior to free weights for myriad of reasons, especially for athletes.

There are specific situations in which machines might be beneficial, namely rehab for injured athletes or when working with athletes who are hyper-mobile in the low back, but these situations are rare and can be addressed on an individual, case-by-case bases. There are some in the strength-training world who will count an increased risk of injury when using free weights as a reason to tout machines—I believe we should start with a solid base of technique and progress from there. I would rather see incoming freshman with no prior weight-room experience lift with light loads using free weights than start out heavier on machines. Teach excellent technique first, then progress; I believe the payoff will be greater on the back end in the junior and senior years.

Compound Lifts > Single-Joint Lifts

This is another general thought that is well established in the strength-training world and, again, needs little explanation here. This is not to say that all single-joint exercises are bad or that all multi-joint exercises good, but, in general, for the purposes of training sprint swimmers, you will get more from multi-joint lifts than from single. As a simple example, consider a free-weight squat versus leg extensions and hamstring curls and the implications for sprint swimming. If we are looking to maximize the distance and speed we push off walls, for example, I would advocate for a squat over the single-joint lifts. Not only are we adhering to the principle of specificity more closely, we are further increasing testosterone levels in the process, for we know that compound lifts do so much better than single-join exercises.

As another example, we love the deadlift here at Liberty, and more specifically we prefer the trap-bar deadlift over the straight-bar for our athletes. I believe in the benefits of the trap bar for athletes to such a degree that it was one of the first questions I asked when I helped interview Shelton for our vacant strength-coach position last summer. The question was simply this: "Do you favor straight or trap bar for athletes?"

I was sold when, without hesitation, he replied, "Absolutely trap bar." And the rest was history. I cannot recall exactly what he said to follow up, but it mattered little, for we were on the same page in regards to deadlifting, and when a swimming coach and strength coach are on the same page in regards to deadlifts, all is well in the world.

In my humble opinion, there is no better exercise to develop total-body general strength and power than the trap-bar deadlift. The benefits to favoring the trap bar over a straight bar for deadlifting are numerous, and I will list just a few:

1. The trap bar is safer, lowering the amount of sheer force placed on the spine.

2. The trap bar is better for beginners—see above—and the technique is easier to learn than that of the straight bar.

3. The trap-bar deadlift actually produces higher peak force and power output than a straight-bar deadlift, a fact that may surprise some readers.

4. The trap bar deadlift is the perfect mix between a squat and a traditional straight-bar deadlift, working the quads a bit more than a straight-bar dead and the hamstrings a bit more than a traditional squat.

5. A trap or hex bar with the extended handle grip is fantastic for taller athletes or for those with low-back or hip-flexibility issues.

Jake Shellenberger

6. When considering the principle of specificity for swimming, specifically, the joint angles achieved in the trap-bar deadlift more closely mimic those seen in the start and in pushing off walls than what we see with the straight-bar deadlift.

7. Trap-bar jumps, while an advanced lift, are fantastic for developing explosive power. These are safer than squat jumps, and I am not sure this lift is possible with a straight bar. I've never seen it attempted, nor do I believe it should be.

8. And the list goes on and on.

When looking at "bang for the buck," so to speak, and efficiency in the weight room, consider that the trap-bar deadlift builds the following muscle groups: quads, hamstrings, glutes, lats, traps, erector spinae, obliques, abdominals, and other muscles of the core. If that were not enough, the forearms and grip strength are also targeted, and last but not least, the trap bar deadlift is one of the best for growth-hormone and testosterone production as well. Consider the above, and then think about the implications for sprint swimming. Yes!

Quite frankly, I find it to be the near-perfect lift, and I would go so far as to say that if I had to choose just one lift to do for the rest of my life to maintain the highest quality of said life, it would without a doubt be the trap-bar deadlift. As I am in retirement-strength-training mode this isn't far off; my personal lifting sessions consist of mainly trap-bar deads, pull-ups, various rows, and a few overhead lifts.

The trap-bar deadlift is one of our core focus lifts here at Liberty, and it was a mainstay during my time at Penn State. Because the lift is safer than a traditional straight-bar dead, it can be used throughout a wide range of programming. For example, we use it as part of a GH-type circuit, with lower weight and higher reps, and we also use it to go heavy and develop maximal strength. As an example of both:

1. As part of a GH-type of circuit a station, we would feature eight repetitions of a trap bar deadlift, at 60-70% of a 1RM, and we would go through the circuit three times.

2. As part of maximum-strength work, we would go three sets of two repetitions approaching 88-90% of a 1RM.

Rate-of-force development and power can also be targeted, as the trap-bar deadlift can be performed faster and safer than a straight-bar deadlift. If you have shied away from deadlifting in your program due to the risk of low-back injury, I would urge you to consider the trap-bar deadlift as an alternative. Talk it over with your strength coach, and pick his or her brain; this exercise comes highly recommended for athletes by elite-level strength coaches, and there is myriad of information and articles across the web and from conferences and professional seminars that outline the many benefits.

To summarize, the trap-bar deadlift is a safe, highly effective, and specific way to hit several of my general thoughts. It raises testosterone and growth hormone levels better than most exercises; it develops general strength and power; it is certainly a compound lift; and, when performed with a trap or hex bar, it is obviously a free-weight exercise. There are machines in the industry that mimic a trap-bar deadlift, and I urge you to steer clear of such devices if you decide to implement this exercise into your program. Moreover, trap-bar deadlifts closely mimic the joint angles and range of motion found in starts and pushing off walls, and this fact should go far in easing the concerns of those in the hard-line principle of specificity camp.

1. **General Strength**
2. **Specific Strength**
3. **In-Water Power**
4. **Free Swimming**

I believe this to be most logical progression when looking at the role of strength training in sprint swimming as a whole. Again, I believe we should start with a wide base of general strength and athleticism. We should then lean toward the principle of specificity and target the muscle groups and/or movements we see in sprint swimming with a more specific approach. In-water power training is then used to "transfer" this general and specific land strength into more specific power in the water that mimics closely the joint angles and movements we see in our sport. Fast, unresisted "free" swimming is the end result.

This entire book is the *how* and some of the *why* of the third stage, and, again, the methods described are the best way I have found over the past ten years to transfer land strength and power into specific power in the water. As for the progression, in regards to general and specific strength, I believe that an athlete with a higher capacity and base amount of general strength will have more "in the tank," so to speak, to apply to the Power Towers and to other power-training gear. He or she will then in turn be faster on the Towers or said gear, as well as in free, untethered swimming.

Correlation and causation debates aside, we have seen time and time again here at Liberty that our fastest sprint athletes, in freestyle and the strokes, are almost always our strongest land athletes, and are almost always our best on the Towers and weight belts. It is extremely rare that we see a sprinter, for example, who is subpar on the Towers or belts but fast in the 50 or 100 of free or stroke. General strength converts to Power Towers, and Power Towers and weight belts convert to free swimming. This progression makes logical sense to me, and, while yes, there are some who will disagree, I do believe that much causation is at play here with regards to land strength, power in the water, and free swimming. This progression simply works, for lack of a better term.

In Summary of General Thoughts

To summarize my general thoughts on strength training for sprint swimming, let me simplify and convert said thoughts to a bullet-point format. As for simplicity, if these guidelines are followed closely, one can benefit from a wide-ranging array of details with regards to specific lifts, rep and load schemes, and other characteristics of the actual programming, if you will. We tend to complicate programming specifics more than needed, and reverting back to simplicity can help us see a big-picture, macro view of the goals of a strength-training program.

1. Start by developing a general base of land strength and athleticism, then move toward specific strength and power.
2. Raise testosterone levels as high as is possible to do in a safe, *legal*, natural manner.
3. Favor free weights over machines.
4. Favor compound lifts over single-joint lifts.

5. Convert land strength to specific in-water power through the various power-training protocols found throughout our sport.

Certainly there is more to it than that, but by following the above guidelines, a strength or swimming coach could fill in the exercise selection and set/rep details to design a great program for sprint swimmers. I believe these general thoughts to be so powerful that I will boldly claim that the details of the programming are secondary and matter less in the development of sprint swimmers than getting these five general thoughts right. I state as much assuming we are not following a HIIT-style program, in which case, the details of the programming need some work!

While I cannot prove the above claim to be true, I see it play out in countless examples across the elite, Division I level year in and year out. Stanford, Cal, Georgia, NC State, Tennessee, Arizona, etc.—all are sprinting at a high level, and all vary in the exercise selection and programming details with which they train their sprinters in the weight room. What they have in common, more often than not, are variations of said general thoughts. These programs feature tall, strong, fit, high-testosterone sprinters, who train primarily with free weights and compound lifts, and who all engage in some form of in-water power training to "convert" that land strength and athleticism to specific power in the water. I believe we can elicit greater improvements from our athletes by focusing on what the aforementioned programs are doing the same, rather than what they are doing differently.

In closing, strength training and overall general athletic development are of high importance for sprint swimming. In the spirit of classical academic and philosophical debate, I would love to see more coaches and sport scientists challenge one another over the merits of strength training for swimming; in my humble opinion, we need more good-natured debate in our sport!

Jake Shellenberger

Chapter 11: Conclusion

"Any work is always improvable, you cannot really finish the work, you can only abandon it out of tiredness or incompetence."

Amit Kalantri

IN FINISHING, please accept a most sincere thank you. I realize my writing style is a bit different than most in the world of sport; I studied history in college, and as writers, we tend to take on the characteristics of those whom we both studied and emulated in our most formative writing years. I wrote extensively in the Shippensburg history program, and for that experience I am thankful; for my readers, perhaps not so much! Writers of history tend to be long-winded, include a few more commas in their works than most, and generally do not mind if their sentence structure borders on that of the infamous run-on; attempt to dissect the preamble of any issue of *Lapham's Quarterly*, for example, in which Lewis H. Lapham regularly pens sentences totaling more than a hundred words and, in a rare feat of literary skill, manages to not just hold, but to captivate the attention of the unsuspecting reader while doing so. I should note that those who devour such works of history love this elevated writing style, and thus the cycle of longer-than-need-be historical writing and higher-than-necessary Gunning Fog Indexes continues. Thankfully those clamoring for short and concise sentence structure did not infiltrate the historical world!

Creating this book was a tremendous learning experience and certainly not an easy task. While I am passionate about Power Towers, power training in general (for all types, not just sprinters), and our beloved sport of swimming as a whole, organizing that passion into a coherent work worth publishing took the better part of nine months and countless hours of research, writing, revising, editing, and more of the same, and, for some readers, labeling this work as coherent would be debatable indeed!

I am left with more questions than I have answers, and, in some ways, that was one of my goals; this work is as much about my own personal

211

Jake Shellenberger

growth as a coach as it is about sharing knowledge with others and contributing to the body of swimming literature, and I would assume that many authors feel the same when they come to the conclusion of a work to which they devote much time, energy, passion, and thought.

The Future of Power Training is Bright

Where are the limits of Power Towers, weight belts, and resistance training in general? We know that more is not always better, but we also know that more of the right training is always better. And what is right? Is resistance training the right way? How can we be sure? Many coaches see fantastic results from resistance work, while some, including Dr. Ernest Maglischo and Dr. Brent Rushall, point to the scientific literature and note that resistance training is not shown to increase performance. While I would respectfully disagree, one certainly will find it a challenge to argue against their respective results, both in the pool and in the lab.

I am obviously a believer in power and resistance training in swimming, and here at Liberty we will continue to push the limits of what is thought possible. Power and resistance training stimulates my mind much more than the various forms of aerobic training, and in writing power sets I am able to fully explore the creativity that accompanies said cognitive stimulation. As we now know, resistance training can be, and certainly is, much more than a few stroke cycles max on a Power Tower or bucket system, and here at Liberty we have proven that what coaches thought was "heavy" for weight belt efforts is actually not.

Imagine where we as a coaching body will be ten, fifteen, and twenty years from now. Will we look back and think twenty-five pounds to be light for a weight belt as I do now with Freas' 1995 recommendation of ten pounds? And of Power Towers, what forms of resistance training will coaches use twenty years from now? I would think the technology of resistance training will continue to advance, and I am excited for the future. Perhaps we see some type of twenty-five-meter cord coming from a computer system with programmable and exact resistance in a small, compact box of some sort? Perhaps I could program said resistance from an application on my iPhone "on the go" as athletes move throughout a workout? I use my iPhone and iPad with the GoPro camera and Coach's Eye app for instant feedback on deck as we speak—surely we could also do this with resistance training? For the strength training gurus in the crowd, imagine a TENDO unit married to a Power Tower in a much smaller contraption—certainly it is possible, and the market is there. Speaking of the GoPro, the new iPhone 7 is rumored to be completely waterproof (the iPhone 6s is waterproof, but is not advertised as such), and this will revolutionize the way coaches view the underwater portion of our sport.

Back to the limits of resistance training, I believe we have much more left in the tank to explore; we simply need the coaches with the creativity and the athletes with the right physics and the right mindsets to fully explore the potential.

I think back to Florent Manaudou's 50 freestyle in London and see the future of fast swimming—a strong, powerful athlete with much height and the wingspan to match holding on to deep water with a .91 tempo and swimming as "big" as is possible for said athlete to swim. Vlad Morozov is another who comes to mind—his 17.86 50 freestyle split at NCAAs in 2013 featured a .83 tempo while holding on to fast water. Would it be possible to train a 6'6" sprinter such as Manaudou to do the same? Certainly, Caeleb Dressel needs no introduction, and his 18.20 NCAA and American record from the 2016 Men's NCAA championship featured a .93 tempo, fantastic front-side underwaters, and a "big" stroke that maximized length and power. Could Dressel's power be enhanced to hold the same stroke length with a .82 tempo, as he had his freshman year with a shorter stroke? And will we see a 17-second flat start 50, if that is indeed possible?

Propulsion vs. Drag Reduction: The Future

Many coaches believe, and the intellectual inertia of our sport perpetuates, that further reducing drag and not focusing on increasing propulsion is the answer to fast swimming in the future, and I respectfully disagree. While drag reduction is important, yes, and all coaches including myself strive to reduce drag, I believe wholeheartedly that the fastest future sprint efforts will simply feature bigger, stronger, more powerful athletes who are able to use said power to maximize their stroke lengths with the fastest tempo possible, while holding on to "hard" water. Runway models do not swim fast; Florent Manaudou does. (Perhaps this is a bad example, as he models some himself, but you get the idea.)

As a simple case in point, revisited again, why are men faster than women? Do they train harder? Do they feature less form and surface drag when moving through the water? Or is it that they are bigger, stronger, and more powerful than their female counterparts? On the opposite side of the same coin, go to a number of local summer-league pools, and you will see that the eight-under girls' records are often faster than the eight-under boys' records. Why is this? And that is why I believe propulsion and specifically the maximizing of power production and power endurance will trump drag reduction in the future of fast swimming.

In another example, consider that Olivia Smoliga of Georgia set the NCAA record in the 50 free with a 21.21 at this year's 2016 NCAA championships. 21.21 is an incredible time, and we are knocking on the door of a sub-21-second women's 50 free. Yet, as fast as that swim is, 21.21 wouldn't even make the NISCA high school boys' all-American list, as a hundred high school boys were 20.88 or faster in the 2015-2016 season, and certainly a great many more were faster than Smoliga's 21.21. In fact, one would have to go back to the 2009-2010 season for Smoliga's time to make the list, where her 21.21 would have tied with five other boys for 127th place that year. Put another way, the all-time fastest NCAA 50 free on the women's side would not have made the top one hundred (and then some) fastest high school boys' times over the past six years. That fact is cognitively invigorating (or it should be) when taken in the context of strength, power, and their importance for fast swimming.

Again, I ask, are these hundreds and hundreds of high school boys working harder than Olivia? Are they receiving better coaching than Smoliga is at Georgia's elite program? Are they better from a purely technical standpoint? Do they minimize drag more efficiently? Do they feature less form or surface drag than Smoliga? What is the biggest factor in why they are faster? And what does that mean for the future of fast swimming?

Why do women who take performance-enhancing drugs such as testosterone and HGH swim faster than they otherwise could without them? Do these women somehow magically reduce more drag after doping? If anything, form and surface drag increase as muscle cross sectional area increases. Yet these drugs are still banned and performances still increase when they are taken. Dr. Rushall doesn't believe swimmers should lift weights, as the research he cites informs him that strength training has no effect on improved swimming performance. Using that logic, we shouldn't ban drugs that improve strength and power and increase muscle fiber cross sectional area, for they have no influence on fast swimming and do not enhance performance, as the research he cites would suggest. Will the authors of the studies he cites be the first in line to recommend relaxing WADA's current rules? While obviously a rhetorical question—why do some still not make the connection?

The Future of Women's Sprint Freestyle

As I coach a women's program, I have a particular interest in the future of women's sprint freestyle, and I imagine said future to be, again, dominated by taller, stronger, more powerful athletes, who are, as with their male counterparts, able to maximize stroke length with the fastest tempo possible while holding water. The simple physics of the matter is that to do so requires more strength and power attached to the longer levers. Dream with me for a second—imagine if our sport could recruit and retain the Brittney Griners of the world, who, at 6'9" and 205 pounds, would make for a sprint coach's dream if she had started out in swimming from five years and so forth. Another WNBA example is Sylvia Fowles of the Minnesota Lynx, who, at 6'6" and 212 pounds, moves like a point guard, not a center. Taller, stronger, more powerful women—I believe this is the future of fast swimming on the women's side, and, again, imagine if we could train a 6'5" female with a higher percentage of fast-twitch muscle fibers to hold a straight-arm stroke that maximizes length with a .90 tempo. It would take quite a bit of strength and power to get the physics right, but I believe we could do it. Take the NCAA DI women's volleyball all-America selections every year, for another example, featuring athletes at 6'3" and so forth with thirty-plus-inch vertical jumps. Imagine that kind of athlete, or hundreds of them across the country, starting out in the pool at age six. We have a lot of improvements left to make, and the better athletes will help us get there.

Elite-level sport, in general, has a habit of weeding out body types that don't belong, and to reiterate a simple case in point from earlier, female runway model body types, at 5'11" and 110 pounds, while perhaps maximizing form and surface drag reduction, don't swim fast, while Chantal Van Landeghem, at 6'4" and 170 pounds, swims quite fast indeed, with personal bests ahead of Rio currently standing at 24.3 and 53.8 in the big pool and 21.7 and 47.4 in the short-course yard format.

I would assume that if we were picking a summer-league relay, school yard style, with two team captains and potential relay members standing on the pool deck, the overwhelming majority of athletes, coaches, and even the sport scientists referenced in Dr. Rushall's studies would pick the Van Landeghem body type over the runway model if they were serious about winning our hypothetical relay. They would pick the body type, instinctively perhaps, not quite sure why they were doing it, but they would pick 6'4" 170-pound over a 5'11" 110-pound regardless of what their antiquated research told them.

Amy Van Dyken, Jenny Thompson, Inge de Bruijn, Britta Steffen, Libby Trickett, Dara Torres, Therese Alshammar, Inge Dekker, Femke Heemskerk, Marleen Veldhuis, Ranomi Kromowidjojo, Amanda Weir, Simone Manuel, and the list goes on and on. All are elite sprint women for their time (and some still are), and all have or had body types that we know didn't shy away from the weight room, body types that you would pick for your summer-league relay, regardless of what the research said about strength training and how it relates to fast swimming.

Consider that Van Dyken went 21.77 in the 50 free way back in 1994, a time that would have finaled at every NCAA championship since then, and will for the foreseeable future. Consider also that even at the height of the suit era, in 2009, Van Dyken's 21.77 still would have placed her second at the NCAA championships, a testament to her strength, power, and dominance in the SCY format. Should sprint swimmers, especially women, strength train in order to maximize performance? One would think that if the answer were no, we as a collective body of coaches would have figured out as much by now, or those respective body types who did not strength train or who were not naturally strong would have found their way to the top of the podium en masse, whether at the elite NCAA level or beyond.

Closing

In closing, thank you again for reading. I enjoy sharing my love and passion for our sport and specifically for power and sprint training, and again you can find more sets, complete workouts, and thoughts on my website at www.jakeshell.com, along with supplemental material to this book. My hope is that you have learned and unlearned much and that you will take the ideas shared here and improve upon them in your own program. Question them, attack them, work and rework them in your mind or on paper, and then make them your own and make them better. Ask the students of the sport in your program how they would improve the various sets and theories. Have fun experimenting while realizing your creativity by fully exploring the Power Towers and other tools for resistance training, and together let us expand on the limited knowledge that we have in this area.

There is much more to the Power Tower and other forms of resistance than simply going max for a 12.5-yard effort or a few stroke cycles, and I believe wholeheartedly that our athletes have much to gain from our collective ingenuity. I am excited for the future of our sport and how this work might impact sprint training specifically; I would be delighted, for example, if this book inspired or in some way aided the first sub-18.00 and 21.00 50-yard freestyle performances.

Jake Shellenberger
Lynchburg, VA
July 2016

Jake Shellenberger

References

Beautiful sport moments for NL. "Inge de Bruijn Gold 50m Freestyle 2004 Athens Olympics." Filmed 2004. YouTube video, 1:33. Posted July 2009. https://youtu.be/NIs_gtOLOp8.

Colwin, Cecil. 2002. *Breakthrough Swimming.* Champagne: Human Kinetics.

Freas, Samuel James. 2015. *Sprinting II: It Takes Guts.* [City]: Sports-Aid International, Incorporated.

Meade Jr., Thomas A. 1976. "A New Approach and Method of Weight Training for Swimmers." *Swimming Technique* [volume]: [page range].

Swim Swam Partners, LLC. 2015. "Race Video: Watch Jack Conger Break The American Record in the 200 Yard Butterfly." https://swimswam.com/race-video-watch-jack-conger-break-the-american-record-in-the-200-yard-fly-unshaved.